REPORT NO. 13

THE NEGRO
IN THE TOBACCO INDUSTRY

by

HERBERT R. NORTHRUP

Professor of Industry
and
Director, Industrial Research Unit

with the assistance of
ROBERT I. ASH

Published by

INDUSTRIAL RESEARCH UNIT, DEPARTMENT OF INDUSTRY
Wharton School of Finance and Commerce
University of Pennsylvania

Distributed by

University of Pennsylvania Press
Philadelphia, Pennsylvania 19104

Foreword

In September 1966, the Ford Foundation announced a major grant to the Industrial Research Unit of the Wharton School to fund studies of the Racial Policies of American Industry. The purpose of the research effort, now in its fourth year, is to determine why some industries are more hospitable to the employment of Negroes than are others, and why some companies within the same industry have vastly different racial employment policies, and to propose appropriate policy.

The studies have proceeded on an industry-by-industry basis, under the direction of the undersigned, with Dr. Richard L. Rowan, Associate Professor of Industry, as Associate Director. This study of the tobacco industry is the thirteenth in a series of reports dealing with specific industries; others already published include the automobile, aerospace, steel, hotel, petroleum, rubber tire, chemical, and paper industries. Studies of the banking and meat industries are in press; those of the insurance industry and public utilities are in the pre-press editing stage. Among the studies expected to be completed at an early date are those pertaining to coal mining, shipbuilding, motor, rail, air, and urban transit, and department stores. We expect also to send to press shortly major studies combining the findings of the various industries. This report will be included in the book, *Negro Employment in Southern Industry.*

This study covers the industry in which the author did his first published research—"The Tobacco Workers' International Union," *Quarterly Journal of Economics,* November 1942; and Chapter IV of *Organized Labor and the Negro,* Harper, 1944. In turning again to this interesting industry, he received valuable assistance from a former student, Robert I. Ash, who in 1967, wrote his advanced study project in partial fulfillment of the Master of Business Administration degree at the Wharton School on "Racial Employment Practices in the Tobacco Industry." Additional statistical assistance was provided by three other students: John C. Howard, Leslie O. Southgate, Jr., and William S. Swift, and by our permanent editorial staff, Mrs. Marjorie C. Denison and Miss Elsa Klemp. The manuscript was

edited by Mrs. Marie R. Keeney and typed by Mrs. Veronica
Kent, Mrs. Rose Elkin, and Mrs. Marie P. Spence. Mrs. Mar-
garet E. Doyle, Administrative Assistant of the Industrial Research Unit, cared for the numerous administrative details associated with this and all other of the Unit's activities. A special
note of thanks is due the officials of the tobacco companies and
unions who so generously gave their time to answer the author's
queries and to supply information to him. Errors or shortcom-
ings are, of course, the sole responsibility of the author.

In most previous reports, as in this one, the data cited as "in
the possession of the author" have been carefully authenticated
and are on file in our Industrial Research Unit library.

HERBERT R. NORTHRUP, *Director*
Industrial Research Unit
Wharton School of Finance and Commerce
University of Pennsylvania

Philadelphia

April 1970

TABLE OF CONTENTS

LIST OF TABLES

CHAPTER I

Introduction

The tobacco industry has employed Negroes since its inception in colonial Virginia. This study is primarily concerned with the course of Negro employment and industry racial policies in those branches of the industry processing, manufacturing, selling, and distributing cigarettes and "manufactured tobacco"—that is, smoking and chewing tobacco and snuff. Throughout this study, this will be known as the "tobacco industry," as distinct from the "cigar industry." The latter involves quite different manufacturing processes, industrial location, and industry policies, and is included in this study only incidentally. Our concern is with the industry which has had the longest continuous record of factory employment of Negroes in the United States, and which is today concentrated not only in the three southern states of Kentucky, North Carolina, and Virginia, but within these states, in seven cities—Louisville, Kentucky; Durham, Greensboro, Reidsville, and Winston-Salem, North Carolina; and Petersburg and Richmond, Virginia.

An analysis of the racial policies of the tobacco industry affords an opportunity to analyze the impact on such policies, over a long period of time, of such factors as the southern location, employment opportunities following new products and new technologies, mechanization and automation, union attitudes and policies, and governmental restraints. In order to put these matters into perspective, the characteristics of the industry and its structure will be briefly decribed in Chapter II.

CHAPTER II

The Tobacco Industry

When Columbus discovered America, he found the natives growing and processing tobacco for smoking, chewing, and snuff. Led by John Rolfe, at Jamestown, the English colonists later found that tobacco culture was their most profitable enterprise. A large part of the wealth of colonial Virginia and Maryland, and later of other states of the upper South, was based upon export of tobacco, which by the Revolution was about 100 million pounds.[1]

As tobacco was grown in various colonies and in the West Indies, it became apparent that different soils and climates caused many and noticeable differences in the characteristics of the product. The varying properties of the leaf were conducive to its use in many manufactured forms. This realization gave impetus to the importance of the domestic manufacturing of tobacco.

By 1790, 29 million pounds were used in manufacturing by small factories. The product was in the form of a roll or twist from which a portion was cut for chewing or smoking or grated for snuff. The manufacture of cigars began in the early 1800's. Initially, imported Cuban leaf was used, but then domestic products, grown first in Massachusetts and Connecticut and later in Pennsylvania and Wisconsin, were combined with the Cuban imports.[2]

During the first half of the nineteenth century, tobacco manufacturing was concentrated in Virginia and North Carolina. Negro slaves were the principal form of labor. Their masters, the upper class plantation proprietors and some of the bourgeoisie, hired them out to the tobacco manufacturers.[3]

---

1. U.S. Department of Agriculture, Consumer and Marketing Service, *Tobacco in the United States*, Miscellaneous Publication No. 867 (Washington: Government Printing Office, 1966), pp. 1-2.

2. *Ibid.*

3. The extent of Negro labor in these early factories is examined in Chapter III.

CIGARETTES AND THE PRODUCTION PROCESS

Prior to the Civil War, cigarettes were either unknown or confined to use by a small segment of society. They were introduced from Europe soon after the war and Negroes were taught to make them by hand rolling after the industry first experimented using immigrant Jews. By 1884, however, a cigarette machine was introduced which could produce 120,000 cigarettes per day as compared with 2,500, at most, by a hand operator. White, largely female, machine operators replaced Negro hand operators, as has so often been the case, with Negroes remaining in the processing (premanufacturing) jobs. A racial-occupational segregation pattern gradually became rigid. The following detailed description describes how it has operated over the years and explains the work traditionally performed by men and women, blacks and whites. Today, most of the hand operations have been eliminated. The racial-occupational segregation pattern began to crumble in the 1960's.

In the manufacture of cigarettes, four major departments are of importance in characterizing the work for men and women, whites and Negroes. These are the leaf handling, making, packing, and boxing departments. The tobacco leaf that goes into the cigarette is delicate and requires careful and skilled attention. From harvesting to the finishing process, a period ranging from a year to three years may elapse.

The leaf is first removed from the auction room.[4] This was traditionally a male Negro job. The redrying machine was originally operated by white men and the tobacco was fed into it by Negro men. Now this process is largely automatic. Going to a

---

4. The auctioned tobacco is obtained from the following areas: Burley tobacco, 90 percent of which is used in the domestic production of cigarettes, is grown principally in Kentucky and Tennessee, although Ohio, Indiana, Virginia, North Carolina, West Virginia, and Missouri also produce this product. Flue-cured tobacco, 95 percent of which is used in American cigarettes and the rest for smoking and chewing tobaccoes, is grown in Virginia, North Carolina, South Carolina, Georgia, Alabama, and Florida.

Maryland broadleaf, a light air-cured tobacco similar to burley, is used predominantly in cigarettes. Fired-cured, found in Virginia, Tennessee, and Kentucky, is utilized in making snuff, roll, and plug chewing tobacco, strong cigars, and heavy smoking tobacco.

Dark air-cured tobacco, grown in Kentucky, Tennessee, and Virginia, is used mainly for chewing tobacco and snuff, but, to some extent, for smoking tobacco and cigars. Pennsylvania, Wisconsin, and Connecticut grow cigar leaf tobacco. (U.S. Department of Agriculture, *op. cit.*, pp. 3-5.)

cooling chamber, the tobacco is packed into hogsheads and stored in the warehouses, usually by Negro men. This rehandling process is frequently carried on outside the large factory in separate establishments which are open for three or four months only, following the tobacco season. To preserve the tobacco, a large supply of labor must be readily available at this season. At the end of the season, these rehandling plants close down.

After aging, the tobacco is taken to the factory for the first stages of preparation. Negro women traditionally performed the next operations. Before mechanization the "pickers" opened up the "hands" of tobacco or untied the bunched tobacco to pick out the trash or gave it a shake to remove dust before putting it on the moving belt. The "orderers" took up the leaves, tied them in bunches, and hung them on racks before they went into the steamer. Today this is a highly mechanized operation, but Negro women still predominate.

The moist leaves are then ready for stemming. Formerly "shakers" removed and shook out the leaves and placed them on trays. After "sorters" arranged them by size and spread them out, the leaf was ready to stem. Originally done by hand, this is now almost completely mechanized. It has always been a female job.

In hand stemming, which, as indicated, was done almost exclusively by Negro men and women, but very largely by women, the mid rib was deftly removed with the least possible damage to the leaf. In machine stemming, a knife cuts out the vein and the leaves must be so stacked as to avoid damage. The machine at first required an operator, two feeders, and two searchers, but gradually improved mechanization reduced the complement. One of the "feeders" fed to the belt, and the other to the machine. The "searchers" watched the strips as they returned from the machine to complete the stemming if the machine had failed to remove the stem entirely. They also watched the stems to prevent leaves from being taken along with the stems.

The leaves are next prepared for blending and flavoring. This has been a Negro male job and has been regarded as skilled. If for cigarettes, the leaf then goes to the cutting machine, which was traditionally fed by a Negro man, and is shredded to the desired fineness. If the leaves are for smoking or chewing tobacco, the process varies from the point of stemming.

The shredded tobacco is then sent to the making machines, traditionally operated by white women. The "feeder" keeps the shredded tobacco flowing evenly into the machines which roll it in paper. The operator of the machine has traditionally been a white man or woman depending, to some extent, upon the machine. The "catcher" receives the made cigarettes in a tray to be sent to the packing room. The foremen, inspectors, and mechanics have been white men. The "weighers," who test the weight of the cigarettes, and the "counters" have traditionally been white women. The sweepers and cleaners are Negro men. As a rule the white and Negro workers were engaged in different operations and were on different floors or in different buildings.

The various operations of packing have also been jobs for both white men and women. The cigarettes are wrapped in foil, packed, sealed, and labelled by machine, and the revenue stamp affixed. "Watchers" for defective packages, "labelers," "stampers," "belt feeders" who send cartons to be wrapped, "salvagers" and "repairers" who remove parts of damaged packages all have been traditionally white men or women.

The process after stemming varies somewhat for smoking, chewing, and snuff tobacco. For chewing, the tobacco is flavored with mixtures which include licorice, cane sugar, and molasses. This was a job traditionally held by Negro men and women who had some skill. The weighers and dividers who prepared it for the mould were traditionally white as were workers who put on the outside leaf wrapper and operated the hydraulic pressure which gives shape to the plugs. The plugs are tagged and packed into wooden boxes, a job once reserved for white women. In the auxiliary work of making box containers and in removing these boxes for shipment to the market, Negro men have been used.[5]

Negroes historically have done the janitorial, porter, and outside work; whites have held the skilled maintenance jobs. Except for these groups, the segregation has been quite complete, not only occupationally, but also physically. Most Negroes have been employed in the stemming, blending, and shredding departments, which, because of atmospheric requirements, are housed in separate buildings, or at least on separate floors from other operations.

---

5. This outline is essentially an updating of the excellent description found in Charles S. Johnson, "The Tobacco Worker," National Recovery Administration, Division of Review, Industrial Studies Section, 1935, 2 vols., MS in U. S. Archives, Washington, D. C. (copy in author's possession), Vol. I, pp. 14-17.

INDUSTRIAL CHARACTERISTICS

Table 1 sets forth employment, payrolls, capital expenditures, and other industrial data for the various subdivisions of the tobacco industry for 1967 by the federal government's standard industrial classification system (SIC) of data collection. These data, first of all, make it very clear that the tobacco industry is not a large employer, having only 75,000 employees in 1967, according to the Census of Manufactures.[6] About two-thirds of these are in the branches of the industry covered by this study.

The cigarette sector of the industry is by far the largest employer, the chewing, smoking, and snuff (manufactured tobacco) sector, which has been declining on a secular basis for many years, the smallest. Tobacco stemmeries and redrying facilities include two types: manufacturers (captive) and independents. The former are owned by the manufacturing companies and operated for their own use throughout the year according to their needs in the manufacture of the products. Thus, despite some seasonal variations, these stemmeries provide year around employment for their workers, most of whom are Negroes.

Independent stemmeries, on the other hand, are operated by leaf tobacco dealers, the middlemen who purchase "green" leaf tobacco from farmers and sell it to manufacturers. These leaf dealers also age and redry tobacco and stem it for smaller companies and for export. Some of the leaf dealers have large storage facilities and can operate all year around, but most of them confine their operations to the late summer and fall months after the tobacco crop has been harvested.

Tobacco stemmeries are located in small towns throughout the tobacco-growing regions. They employ about twice as many persons—mostly Negro women—at peak season as they do on average during a year. About 90 percent of the employment in stemmeries serving the non-cigar tobacco industry is found in Kentucky, North Carolina, and Virginia.[7]

Tobacco manufacturing is today a highly mechanized series of operations. Payrolls are relatively small, cost of materials and value added by manufacturing are high. As will be shown

---

6. Census of Manufactures data are constructed quite differently from those of the U. S. Bureau of Labor Statistics, utilized below, and the two are not comparable.

7. Herbert R. Northrup, *Organized Labor and the Negro* (New York: Harper & Bros., 1944), pp. 108-109.

TABLE 1. *Tobacco Industry*
Employment, Payroll, Capital Expenditures, and Other Data
by Standard Industrial Classification, 1967

	Tobacco Industry (SIC 21)	Cigarettes (SIC 2111)	Cigars (SIC 2121)	Chewing and Smoking Tobacco (SIC 2131)	Tobacco Stemming and Redrying (SIC 2141)[a]
			Thousands of Employees		
All employees	75	37	19	4	15
			Millions of Dollars		
Payroll	377	219	73	22	63
Value added by manufacture	2,011	1,615	199	89	108
Cost of materials	2,898	1,385	177	66	1,270
Value of shipments	4,957	3,036	374	156	1,391
Capital expenditures, new	53	32	5[b]	2	14

Source: *U. S. Census of Manufacturers, 1967*, Series MC 67(P)-1, Summary Series, Preliminary Report, April 1969.

[a] Data subject to further checking and revision.

[b] Limited reliability.

in the examination of the racial employment trends in the industry, the trend since the development of the cigarette machine until recent years has featured increased productivity which permitted greater production either without materially adding to employment or actually reducing employment. In recent years, at least until 1960, Negroes have been disproportionately affected by these trends.

Industrial Structure

The development of the cigarette-making machine changed the industry from one of small shops to one in which the economies of scale all but eliminated the small producer. James B. Duke materially aided the process. In the age of trusts he had welded together by 1890 nearly all cigarette manufacturing except R. J. Reynolds, and the bulk of manufactured tobacco [8] into one great combine, The American Tobacco Company.

In 1911, The American Tobacco Company was dissolved by order of the United States Supreme Court.[9] The four successor companies are still a dominant part of the tobacco industry almost 60 years later. R. J. Reynolds, American Tobacco (which has changed its name to American Brands to reflect its broader product range), P. Lorillard, and Liggett & Myers were the "Big Four" of the industry until the latter two were passed in sales by Brown & Williamson, a subsidiary of British-American Tobacco Company, and by Philip Morris.

These six companies produced all but a tiny fraction of American-made cigarettes in 1969, as shown in Table 2. (They also produced an overwhelming, but somewhat smaller percentage of all the manufactured tobacco in the United States.) Reynolds and American together produced more than one-half of the 513.3 billion cigarettes sold in 1969. At the other end of the scale, small independent companies held a minute market share, accounting for just 0.3 percent of all the cigarettes sold. The other four major companies each held between about 6 and 15 percent of the sales.

---

8. Duke failed to achieve a similar monopoly in the cigar industry, which remained a handicraft operation with little or no economies of scale until the development of the cigar-making machine around World War I. He secured control of R. J. Reynolds a few days before the Supreme Court ordered his combine dissolved, but never had effective control of this company.

9. *United States* v. *American Tobacco Company*, 221 U. S. 106 (1911).

TABLE 2.   *Tobacco Industry*
Domestic Cigarette Sales by Company, 1969

Company	Domestic Sales Billions of Cigarettes
R. J. Reynolds	163.6
American Tobacco [a]	108.0
Brown & Williamson [b]	81.3
Philip Morris	77.1
P. Lorillard [c]	47.0
Liggett & Myers	35.0
All others	1.3
Total	513.3

Source: *Business Week*, December 13, 1969, p. 82.

[a] Name changed to American Brands in 1969.

[b] Subsidiary of British-American Tobacco.

[c] Absorbed by Loew's Theaters, 1968.

Table 3 sets forth statistics for five of the six major tobacco companies, those for Brown & Williamson, the number three producer, not being available. All are giant corporations and are taking on more and more the aspects of conglomerates. In recent years, for example, R. J. Reynolds acquired McLean Industries, Inc., operators of Sea-Land Service, and P. Lorillard merged into Lowe's Theaters. Philip Morris, Liggett & Myers, and American are all actively expanding into other areas, spurred by the continuing attacks on smoking as a cause of cancer, heart, and respiratory diseases, and the consequent decline in cigarette and tobacco sales.

The data in Table 3 thus reflect corporate activity in areas other than tobacco products. Nevertheless, they again demonstrate the industry's relatively small employment in relation to invested capital and sales. Of the companies, R. J. Reynolds, the only one with headquarters where its main operations are, is the largest and most profitable.

In addition to the six major concerns, there are a number of thriving smaller ones. Such companies are found mostly in the manufactured tobacco segment of the industry, and in the independent processing business. They, like the majors, are located primarily in Virginia, North Carolina, and Kentucky and follow the same general employment policies.

TABLE 3. *Five of the Six Major Tobacco Companies, 1968 Statistics*

Company and 1968 Rank Among Industrial Corporations	Headquarters	Sales	Assets	Net Income	Invested Capital	Number of Employees	Net Income as a Percent of	
							Sales	Invested Capital
		Thousands of Dollars						
R. J. Reynolds (74)	Winston-Salem, N. C.	1,264,681	1,197,107	150,045	938,609	21,332	11.9	16.0
American Tobacco (85)	New York	1,117,419	1,512,061	92,911	712,100	40,540 [a]	8.3	13.0
Philip Morris (147)	New York	675,408	786,578	48,866	314,496	20,000	7.2	15.5
Liggett & Myers (219)	New York	438,248	507,385	24,066	318,104	8,265	5.5	7.6
P. Lorillard (255)	New York	359,180	363,363	30,714	209,586	7,000	8.4	14.3

Source: *Fortune*, Vol. LXXIX (May 15, 1969), pp. 170-177.

Note: Data include non-tobacco business. Since 1968, Reynolds has acquired McLean Industries, the 29th largest transportation company, Lorillard has been acquired by Loew's Theaters, and American Tobacco has changed its name to American Brands, Inc. Data for Brown & Williamson, the number three producer, are not available.

[a] *Fortune* figure may be an error. Tobacco employment in 1968 was about 14,000.

Industrial Location

The history of the tobacco industry has been one of steady industrial concentration of factories into the seven cities of three southern states. In the late twenties and early thirties, Liggett & Myers and American Tobacco abandoned their New York and Philadelphia plants and concentrated their production in the South. The last major northern plant was closed in 1956 when P. Lorillard moved its operations from Jersey City, New Jersey, to Greensboro, North Carolina. Table 4 lists the major company

TABLE 4. *Tobacco Industry*
Major Plant Locations
and Negro Percent of Population Estimates
1965 and 1970

City and State	Estimated Negro Population Percentage		Companies with Major Facilities[a]
	1965	1970	
Louisville, Kentucky	21	24	American[b] Brown & Williamson P. Lorillard Philip Morris
Durham, North Carolina	36	36	American Liggett & Myers
Greensboro, North Carolina	28	30	P. Lorillard
Reidsville, North Carolina	34[c]	35[c]	American
Winston-Salem, North Carolina	36	34	R. J. Reynolds Brown & Williamson
Petersburg, Virginia	47	49	Brown & Williamson
Richmond, Virginia	47	51[d]	American Liggett & Myers Philip Morris

Source: Company annual reports and The Center for Research in Marketing, Inc., *The Negro Population: 1965 Estimates and 1970 Projections* (Peekskill, New York: The Center, 1966).

[a] Excludes stemmeries and warehouses or cigar factories not associated with other plants.

[b] American announced the closing of its Louisville facilities in late 1969; it will concentrate production in other areas.

[c] Author's estimates. In 1960 Negro population was 33 percent of total.

[d] The City of Richmond is now litigating the annexation of certain contiguous areas. An effect could be a reduction in the over-all percentage of Negroes in the city.

plant locations and the estimated percentage of the Negro population in each for 1965 and 1970. Obviously, the industry is concentrated in areas where a sizeable proportion of Negroes dwell and are available for employment.

The degree of concentration of the industry in these three states in terms of employees is shown in Table 5. In 1967, two-thirds of all tobacco workers and over 90 percent of cigarette employees were employed in the three southern states, with North Carolina accounting for more than one-half of the tristate employment. Data for manufactured tobacco and tobacco stemming and redrying are not available, but 80-90 percent of employees in these industry branches are certainly also located in the three states. Indeed, the only significant group of non-cigar tobacco employees not found in Kentucky, North Carolina, and Virginia are the central office employees in New York City, where all the major domestic companies except Reynolds maintain corporate headquarters.

MANPOWER

The tobacco industry, as already noted, is not a large employer. Moreover, as Table 6 shows, employment in several branches has actually declined in many periods as a result of technology or habit changes. For example, between 1919 and 1939, the production index of the cigarette industry (with 1929=100) rose from 43.4 to 147.7; but so great was the increase in productivity, that the employment index fell from 131.5 to 101.7 during this period.[10]

In more recent years, employment in the cigarette sector has increased, although declining cigarette sales in the last two or three years have apparently reversed this trend; employment for a number of years in the cigar branch has declined precipitously; that in manufactured tobacco has continued a long secular decline; and that in tobacco stemming and redrying has also declined. With Negroes concentrated in the latter two branches or in jobs in the cigarette industry that have been easy to automate, these trends have been inimical to Negro employment. The recent decline in cigarette smoking may reduce employment in that sector of the industry in the future.

---

10. U. S. Department of Labor, Wage and Hour Division, "The Tobacco Industry" (Mimeo., 1941), pp. 92-93.

TABLE 5. *Tobacco Industry*
Total Industry and Cigarette Employment
United States and Major Tobacco Manufacturing States, 1967

	Tobacco Industry (SIC 21)	Cigarettes (SIC 211)	Percent of Total Employment in Tobacco Industry	Percent of Total Employment in Cigarettes
Kentucky	13,000	9,400	14.9	22.5
North Carolina	30,700	19,200	35.2	46.1
Virginia	14,500	9,600	16.6	23.0
Total	58,200	38,200	66.7	91.6
Total United States	87,300	41,700	100.0	100.0

Source: U.S. Bureau of Labor Statistics, *Employment and Earnings Statistics for the United States, 1909-68*, Bulletin 3, No. 1312-6 (Washington: Government Printing Office, 1968); and *ibid.*, *Employment and Earnings Statistics for the States and Selected Areas, 1939-67*, Bulletin 180, No. 1370-5 (Washington: Government Printing Office, 1968).

Occupational Distribution

Employment in the tobacco industry is heavily production-worker oriented. Thus in 1967, almost 86 percent of all tobacco workers and more than 90 percent of all cigarette employees were classified as "production workers." [11]

Table 7 provides a more detailed occupational distribution for employees of the six major companies as of 1968. More than 50 percent of all employees are classified as semiskilled (operatives or lower) with the operative group comprising more than one-third of the total work force. Professional and technical representation in the labor force is very low, with total white collar, buoyed by a large sales force, less than 30 percent of the total.

---

11. Data based on U. S. Bureau of Labor Statistics figures.

TABLE 6. *Tobacco Industry*
Employment by Standard Industrial Classification
Selected Years, 1914-1967

Year	Tobacco Manufacturers (SIC 21)	Cigarettes (SIC 2111)	Cigars (SIC 2121)	Chewing and Smoking Tobacco (SIC 2131)	Tobacco Stemming and Redrying (SIC 2141)
1914	195,694	164,163[a]		31,531	n.a.
1919	172,776	150,633[a]		22,143	n.a.
1923	162,076	142,668[a]		19,408	n.a.
1933	90,790	23,816	56,195[b]	10,779	n.a.
1937	97,851	27,655	58,910	11,286	n.a.
1939	96,035	30,803	54,262	10,970	n.a.
1947	111,782	27,674	47,068	11,139	25,901
1952	93,175	29,342	40,165	7,764	15,904
1954	94,862	29,987	38,494	7,535	18,846
1958	84,467	33,832	29,350	6,348	14,937
1960	81,247	36,513	26,319	4,398	14,017
1961	77,456	36,102	23,415	4,654	13,285
1962	75,966	35,434	22,161	4,649	13,722
1963	77,330	35,568	20,731	4,058	16,973
1964	78,838	34,843	22,988	5,054	15,953
1965	74,555	35,924	21,041	4,437	13,153
1966	72,363	35,602	19,357	4,339	13,065
1967	75,000[c]	37,000	19,000	4,000	n.a.

Source: *U. S. Census of Manufactures:*

1947: Vol. II, *Statistics by Industry*, pp. 147-149 (for 1914-1939).

1963: Vol. II, *Statistics by Industry*, Part 1, pp. 21-3, 21A-6, 21A-7 (for 1947-1963).

1967: Series MC67 (P)-1, Summary Series, **Preliminary Report,** April 1969.

Annual Survey of Manufactures, 1964-1966.

[a] Cigarettes and cigars combined as one industry.

[b] Coverage of "Cigars" was incomplete in 1933.

[c] Includes uncorrected SIC 2141 data.

TABLE 7. *Tobacco Industry*
Employment by Occupational Group
Six Companies, 1968

Occupational Group	All Employees	
	Number	Percent
Officials and managers	4,814	7.6
Professionals	1,473	2.3
Technicians	1,456	2.3
Sales workers	5,411	8.6
Office and clerical	5,658	8.9
Total white collar	18,812	29.7
Craftsmen	6,095	9.6
Operatives	21,781	34.4
Laborers	14,560	23.0
Service workers	2,104	3.3
Total blue collar	44,540	70.3
Total	63,352	100.0

Source: Data in author's possession.

Note: Data include non-tobacco employees employeed by tobacco companies, but overwhelmingly reflect the tobacco occupational distribution.

Female Employment

The tobacco industry almost from its inception employed a considerable number of females and still does. In 1968, for example, over one-third of the more than 60,000 employees of the major companies were females.[12] Much of the work is either light machine tending or requires manual dexterity of a type in which women excel. Female employment has long been a practice in the industry and is likely to continue in view of the nature of the operations.

Wages

The tobacco industry is not a high paying one. Table 8 compares average weekly and hourly earnings of production workers in the industry with those in durable and nondurable goods manufacturing, and with two nondurable groups, food and kindred products and textile mill products. It is apparent that cigar

12. Based on data in the author's possession.

manufacturing is the lowest of the group,[13] with cigarette production worker earnings somewhat above the nondurable goods
average and substantially above textile mill products and cigars,
but just slightly below food and kindred products. (The cigarette data include some lower paid prefabrication wages.) The
all-manufacturing average, buoyed by the high paying durable
goods group, exceeds that of cigarettes or any other nondurable
product represented in Table 8.

Separate data for the manufactured tobacco and stemming
and redrying segments of the industry are not available, but
rates therein have always been substantially lower than in cigarettes. Stemming wages, as those in cigar manufacturing, do
not usually exceed the minimum wage by substantial amounts.
Actually few Negroes have traditionally been employed in cigarette manufacturing, the top earnings sector of the tobacco
industry, execpt in the lower paying prefabricating departments.

The earnings picture in the tobacco industry seems to reflect
a number of factors. Among the most significant are probably
the lack of high skills required, the large number of female jobs,
and the abundance of female and Negro labor available in the
southern locations. On the other hand, with labor costs so small

TABLE 8. *Tobacco and Selected Industries*
Average Weekly and Hourly Earnings
Production Workers, 1968

	Average Weekly Earnings	Average Hourly Earnings
All manufacturing	$122.51	$3.01
Durable goods	132.07	3.19
Nondurable goods	109.05	2.74
Tobacco manufacturers	93.87	2.49
Cigarettes	113.93	3.03
Cigars	75.00	2.00
Food and kindred products	114.24	2.80
Textile mill products	91.05	2.21

Source: *Employment and Earnings*, Vol. 15, No. 9 (March 1969), Table C-2.

---

13. The reasons for the low wages in cigar manufacturing have not been in-
vestigated by this author. The decline in employment noted in Table 6
may well be a key factor, for it involves continued mechanization which
eliminates most of the last vestiges of skill in a once craft occupation.

a percentage of the value added by manufacturing, tobacco companies are paying cigarette manufacturing employees substantially more in wages than are textile manufacturers who are faced with the same general conditions, but who have a much higher proportion of labor costs with which to contend. Related both to relative wages and to the proportion of labor costs in the two industries is, undoubtedly, the general absence of unionization in textile manufacturing and its presence in all but one major company in the tobacco industry.

Unionization

Today nearly all tobacco manufacturers are unionized by one organization—the Tobacco Workers International Union. The outstanding exception is the huge R. J. Reynolds complex in Winston-Salem, North Carolina, which was unionized by the TWIU during World War I and by a rival union during World War II, but which today operates on a nonunion basis.[14] Today, the TWIU has a membership of about 34,000.

Most of the TWIU contracts date from the mid-1930's. Before that period, the union existed only on the fringes of the industry by virtue of making common ground with the small manufacturers. In return for permitting the union label to be placed on products, a few small companies in effect unionized their employees. Twice before the 1930's, the TWIU attempted to organize the major companies and even succeeded at Reynolds during World War I. Its eventual failure there, and later that of a rival union, has left Reynolds nonunion.

As might be expected, the TWIU accepted the racial-occupational segregation pattern by having separate locals on the basis of race. This tended to institutionalize the racial-occupational status quo and make it more difficult for the unionized companies to integrate their work forces in the 1960's. On the other hand, even after the separate locals policy was abandoned by the TWIU, the practice of departmental seniority added to the barriers against equal employment and strong local union autonomy restricted opportunities for change. The story of the union role in affecting Negro employment will be recounted within the appropriate time sequences of the following chapters.

---

14. The history of the TWIU is found in Herbert R. Northrup, "The Tobacco Workers International Union," *Quarterly Journal of Economics*, Vol. LVI (August 1942), pp. 606-626; and Northrup, *Organized Labor and the Negro, op. cit.*, Chapter IV.

CHAPTER III

Negro Employment — from the Colonial Period to 1960

As noted in the previous chapter, Negroes have been employed in the tobacco industry of the South since the colonial period of America—longer than in any other manufacturing industry. This chapter surveys racial employment trends from their colonial inception to 1960.

COLONIAL TIMES TO THE GREAT DEPRESSION

The plantation was, by necessity, a self-sufficient economy which produced to satisfy its own needs and utilized available labor. The tobacco-producing plantations of Virginia realized at an early date that it would be profitable to process some of their products for sale in the colonies, and Negro slaves were trained for this work. The need to be self-sufficient and to market their products locally was greatly magnified when war cut off the colonies from their English markets. Consolidation of duplicating efforts "led to slight commercial ventures with the use of Negroes in the manufactures. Planters who could not economically use all their slaves found it profitable to hire out not only slave laborers but trained slave artisans either to companies or to individual artisans and entrepreneurs. These latter were often to be found at the crossroads or in the small towns." [15]

Negroes trained as pressmen, twisters, stemmers, and "eventually coopers" were in demand in the cities by 1800.[16] Throughout the first half of the Civil War period, they were not only widely used in the tobacco factories of Richmond, Petersburg, and Lynchburg, but made up this labor force almost exclusively until the 1850's, when the "higher prevailing wages paid Negroes

---

15. Raymond B. Pinchbeck, *The Virginia Negro Artisan and Tradesman*, University of Virginia, Phelps-Stokes Fellowship Papers, No. 7 (Richmond: William Byrd Press, Inc., 1926), pp. 45-46.

16. *Ibid.*, p. 54.

are said to have been the cause leading to the employment of white women in the lighter processes of the manufacture of tobacco." [17]

The Virginia tobacco factories employed not only male Negro slaves, but also females, and in addition utilized a large proportion of that Commonwealth's free Negroes, both male and female:

Regardless of sex, and regardless of residence in town or country, one line of employment excelled all others with reference to the number of free Negroes it attracted—namely, the tobacco industry. The history of the cultivation of tobacco in Virginia makes evident the very high place which Negro labor, slave and free, held in this industry. Contrary to his position in the cotton industry, in which he was confined largely to cultivation, the Negro was important in the manufacture, as well as in the cultivation, of tobacco. In its manufacture many women workers were engaged. In the factories of Petersburg, where the women were about half as numerous as men, they worked as stemmers, while the men worked as twisters. According to the report on manufactures in Virginia of the 1860 census, there were at this time 261 tobacco establishments employing 11,382 workers at an annual cost of $2,123,732. At least 2,500 of this number were free Negroes, who lived chiefly in Richmond, Petersburg, and Lynchburg, the leading centers of tobacco manufacture, and who worked side by side with slaves. In Lynchburg most of the free Negroes worked in the tobacco factories during the manufacturing season, "and then," said a public official of that town, "the males do whatever comes in their way the balance of the time." In Farmville likewise the five tobacco establishments absorbed many more free Negroes than did any other line of employment. Richmond factories, for some reason, made so little use of women that during the fifties there were about 125 free Negro washerwomen in Richmond and only thirty-nine in Petersburg. The women of the latter place found their opportunity in tobacco factories rather than as washerwomen.[18]

Professor Jackson also affirms that Richmond was the center of the "slave for hire" market, and that the tobacco factories in this city and nearby Petersburg were principal employers of hired-out slave labor as late as 1860.[19]

In North Carolina and Kentucky, there is little evidence of the use of Negroes in tobacco factories probably because such factories did not exist there at that time. An economic history of slaveholding in North Carolina reports considerable agitation

---

17. *Ibid.*, p. 57. See also pp. 54-58.

18. Luther Porter Jackson, *Free Negro Labor and Property Holding in Virginia* (New York: Atheneum, 1969), pp. 94-95.

19. *Ibid.*, pp. 176-177.

about the use of Negro slaves in cotton mills (but little actual such utilization) and much contracting out of slaves for turpentine harvesting and as building artisans and railroad labor; but it makes no mention of tobacco manufactures.[20] North Carolina's rise to first place in the industry occurred after the cigarette became fashionable, for North Carolina's "bright yellow" tobacco proved especially suited for cigarettes. North Carolina tobacco towns owe their start in manufacturing to the inability of farmers during the Civil War to transport their crop to Richmond and the need to manufacture nearer the source of supply.

Reconstruction and the Advent of Cigarette Manufacturing

The immediate post-Civil War reconstruction era saw no diminution in the utilization of Negroes in Virginia tobacco factories. During the period 1800-1875, according to A. A. Taylor, "Practically all travelers saw the blacks at work in the tobacco factories."[21] Moreover, the introduction of machinery in factories in Virginia did not result in the displacement of blacks by whites. Both men and women worked in these plants, and in some cases Negro and white men worked side by side, but white women were not part of any mixed work force. The supervisors, however, were generally white.[22]

In 1879, a Virginia United States Senator asserted that Negroes constituted "the bulk of the labor used in the manufacture of Virginia's great staple—tobacco." Other officials in this period found Negroes "quite free from trade unionism" and "less liable to strikes and interruptions. . . ." But A. A. Taylor's evidence indicates that Negro tobacco workers attempted to form unions and that strikes for higher wages in tobacco factories were not so uncommon.[23]

A British visitor to Virginia stated of the freed men that "Tobacco seems to be specially their vocation . . . [but] cigars,

---

20. Rosser Howard Taylor, *Slaveholding in North Carolina: An Economic View*, The James Sprunt Historical Publications, Vol. 18 (Chapel Hill: University of North Carolina Press, 1926), pp. 38-40, 42, 74-80.

21. A. A. Taylor, *The Negro in the Reconstruction of Virginia* (Washington: The Association for the Study of Negro Life and History, Inc., 1926), p. 116.

22. *Ibid.*, pp. 116-118.

23. *Ibid.*, pp. 119-120.

it seems, are not made by blacks. It is one of the skilled things that they do not do." [24]

When cigarettes were first introduced from abroad, Negroes appeared about to break through the barrier for similar work. After first experimenting with Jewish immigrants who had learned the trade abroad, American tobacco manufacturers in the South turned to Negroes. But then in the 1880's came the introduction of the cigarette machine which could produce 120,-000 cigarettes per day as compared with 2,500 by the most efficient hand rollers. (Machine production has increased many fold since then.) The tobacco industry, following custom of the day, employed white females as machine operatives, white males as mechanics and set-up men. Whites remained as supervisors and as white collar workers. As machines were developed to make manufactured tobacco (smoking, chewing, and snuff), jobs were likewise divided up on a racial basis. By 1900, the racial-occupational segregation pattern, described in the previous chapter, was thoroughly effectuated in southern tobacco factories.

Although Negro workers lost out in the competition for jobs in the modern tobacco manufacturing processes, they continued to hold a large, and for a long period, increasing share of the total jobs in the industry, once the influx of white machine operators, mechanics, supervisors, and office employees had stabilized. Because of the low wages paid in the stemming and processing jobs, companies made little or no effort to mechanize them prior to 1932. On the other hand, mechanization in the cigarette manufacturing area, and mechanization and declining demand in the manufactured tobacco sector, tended either to restrain advances in the white-designated jobs or even to reduce the number of such jobs. In addition, the economies of large scale, the consolidations effected by the "tobacco trust" and its successor companies, and the impetus given the industry to move South in order to maximize the advantages of nearness to raw materials and of cheap labor, all tended to increase job opportunities for Negroes during the last decades of the nineteenth and first ones of the twentieth centuries.

Both the traditional headquarters of the industry—Richmond, Virginia—and the newer industrial cities of North Carolina and Kentucky were well ensconced as tobacco manufacturing centers before the turn of the century. Thus a reporter noted in 1899:

---

24. Quoted by *ibid.*, p. 118.

The colored people of Richmond are employed principally in all branches of the tobacco business, with the exception of cigarette making, cigar making and cheroot rolling. About 8,000 men, women and children are employed in the factories; of this number about 2,000 might be classified as skilled laborers.[25]

According to Greene and Woodson, "Negro workers increased, too, with the spread of this industry into North Carolina, Kentucky and Missouri. Among the centers of the industry were Winston-Salem, Durham, Louisville and St. Louis, where about two-thirds of the employees were Negroes."[26] Tradition was a factor in maintaining these jobs for Negroes (as well as denying them jobs in cigarette factories), but poor working conditions—dust particles and humid atmosphere—and low wages contributed also. Nevertheless, it remained for Negroes virtually the only significant factory work and factory employer of women in the South prior to World War I.

World War I to the Great Depression

By and large, Negroes maintained their position in the tobacco industry during the first three decades of the twentieth century. The continued increase in cigarette sales was largely offset by improved equipment so that employment in cigarette manufacturing did not increase. On the other hand, the processing work for that manufacturing remained low paid, largely hand labor performed by Negroes. As the demand for tobacco products— mainly cigarettes—grew, the need for more processing labor increased. Moreover, the remaining major plants in the North, with only a few exceptions, were closed and consolidated in the South by 1930. Finally, the demand for labor during World War I brought proportionately more opportunities for whites than Negroes, and tended to reinforce the dependence of tobacco companies on Negroes for the processing work, with Negro women in the South having, by 1930, still very few, if any, manufacturing job opportunities elsewhere.

Table 9 shows the number and proportion of operatives and laborers in the three principal tobacco manufacturing states,

25. *Proceedings, Hampton Conference*, July 1902, p. 43, quoted by Lorenzo J. Greene and Carter G. Woodson, *The Negro Wage Earner* (Washington: The Association for the Study of Negro Life and History, Inc., 1930), p. 152.

26. Greene and Woodson, *loc. cit.* St. Louis has since lost its position in the industry.

TABLE 9. *Tobacco Industry*
Laborer and Operative Employment by Race
Major Tobacco Manufacturing States, 1910-1930

	1910			1920			1930		
	Total	Negro	Percent Negro	Total	Negro	Percent Negro	Total	Negro	Percent Negro
Kentucky	8,896	4,046	45.5	14,719	8,521	57.9	7,006	3,534	50.4
North Carolina	7,735	5,716	73.9	20,006	14,852	74.2	19,756	15,049	76.2
Virginia	12,397	8,948	72.2	15,520	10,457	67.4	11,104	7,142	64.3
Total	29,028	18,710	64.5	50,245	33,830	67.3	37,866	25,725	67.9

Source: *U. S. Census of Population:*

1910: Vol. IV, *Occupations,* Table 7.
1920: Vol. IV, *Occupations,* Table 1.
1930: Vol. IV, *Occupations,* Table 11.

1910-1930. More than 90 percent of all Negroes in the non-cigar tobacco industry were then, as now, found in these three states. Although these data include a few cigar workers, the number producing cigars in these states has been insignificant.

On the other hand, the proportion of Negroes in the tobacco industry during these twenty years was less than is indicated by Table 9. The term "operative" as then defined by the census excludes certain highly skilled personnel as well as supervisory, managerial, and other salaried groups, nearly all of whom were then white. Thus in 1930, when 67.9 percent of the laborers and operatives in these states were black, only 58.7 percent of all gainful workers (that is, those employed or actively seeking work) were Negro. Nevertheless, in view of the overwhelming proportion of the work force of the industry that is classified as "production," "operative," or "semiskilled," the data in Table 9 do present a good picture of the racial employment trends for the period.

Looking at Table 9, we find that Negroes actually increased their proportion of factory jobs between 1910 and 1930, especially during the first of these two decades. The most substantial proportional increase came in Kentucky between 1910 and 1920, but was lost there during the following decade when black workers were disproportionately hurt in an exodus of work from Kentucky. In terms of numbers of jobs, North Carolina tripled both its tobacco work force and its Negro work force between 1910 and 1920, and then during the next decade added slightly to its black tobacco worker complement while its total work force declined slightly. In Virginia, both the total work force and the Negro work force increased slightly between 1910 and 1920, but in the following decade, both the total work force and the Negro proportion thereof suffered losses of jobs.

The principal reasons for these racial employment trends have already been noted. One was the continued decline in the sales and the production of manufactured tobacco. More significant was the consolidation of the industry in the three southern states. About four-fifths of the tobacco factories operating in 1914 were closed by the middle of the next decade; the number of tobacco workers declined by 178,872 in 1914 to 132,132 in 1925; the number of establishments declined from 13,951 to 2,623. While this occurred, value of product sold increased from $490 million to nearly $1.1 billion.[27]

---

27. *Ibid.*, pp. 287-288 quoting U. S. Department of Commerce, *Statistical Abstract of the United States*, 1926, p. 749.

Although most of these changes reflect the development of new cigar-making equipment, they also include the impact of continued consolidation of plants and mechanization in the cigarette manufacturing sector. More facilities were abandoned in the North than in the South. Meanwhile continued mechanization occurred in the cigarette sector of the industry:

Using 1929 as a base of 100, the index of output per wage earner per year in the cigarette branch rose from 32.8 in 1920 to 112.8 in 1930 and that of output per man-hour, from 28.7 to 105.3. Although the production of cigarettes increased from 47.4 billion in 1920 to 123.8 billion in 1930, the percentage increase in production was less than that in labor productivity. Thus the rate of mechanization not only prevented the cigarette branch from compensating for the decline in employment due to the decrease in the production of manufactured tobacco, but it was also so rapid that it caused unemployment within the cigarette branch itself.[28]

While this was occurring, the segregated Negro work areas paid such low wages that for them laborsaving equipment was either not economical or not even considered.[29]

During these two decades the Women's Bureau of the U. S. Department of Labor made a number of studies of the tobacco industry. It reported that the racial-occupational pattern was fixed and strong; that the clean, machine work was performed by white women whose "working conditions and wages were in striking contrast to those of Negro women workers. Their separation and isolation to prevent any contrast was apparent in the 16 establishments in which both races were employed." [30]

In regard to the condition of Negro workers, the Women's Bureau reported:

In tobacco factories conditions were particularly unsatisfactory. Sometimes the fumes were so strong that they were stifling and provoked incessant coughing from persons not accustomed to such conditions. Frequently the women wore handkerchiefs tied over their noses and mouths to prevent inhaling the heavy tobacco dust diffused throughout the room. One manager said new workers often suffered from nausea and loss of appetite, but as soon as they got used to the tobacco they did not mind it. Dust was thick in the air in many

28. Herbert R. Northrup, *Organized Labor and the Negro* (New York: Harper & Bros., 1944), pp. 105-106.

29. Tobacco manufacturers told the author in the 1940's that it may well have been economical to install machinery during this period but in view of the low wages of Negroes, they never considered the potential of mechanization.

30. Quoted by Greene and Woodson, *op. cit.*, p. 285.

of the factories, especially those in which the screener was operated in the general workroom without exhaust systems. In 18 factories these conditions were so bad that ventilating systems to purify the air were needed. A strong contrast was noted in one factory; the dust was taken off by electric fans, while humidifiers and a system of washing the air kept it pure and fresh.[31]

As for wages, Negro medians for women were $4.00 to $5.00 per week in the mid-1920's, those of whites as high as $13.20 per week. Hours were long—55 to 60 per week—and employment in the Negro jobs often seasonal.[32]

THE NEW DEAL TO 1960

The thirty-year period between 1930 and 1960 saw whites clearly emerge as the dominant employee group in the tobacco industry. Despite continued increased sales of tobacco products, particularly cigarettes, during this period and further (almost complete) consolidation of the industry in the three southern states, Negro employment declined as a percentage of total employment in each of the three decades. The reasons are indisputable: government imposition of minimum wages, employer response by mechanizing jobs in the stemmeries and in other areas where Negroes were employed, failure on the part of employers and unions to open up jobs in the white sectors of the industry to displaced Negroes, and failure of the dominant union to challenge the status quo in behalf of its eroding black membership.

The NRA Period

In his endeavors to lift the country out of the Great Depression, President Franklin D. Roosevelt obtained legislation, known as the National Industrial Recovery Act, which permitted employers to combine for the purpose of regulating production, wages, and hours under "Codes of Few Competition" or "NRA codes." While the codes were being hammered out, industries were requested to reduce hours, raise wages, and hopefully increase employment. The major tobacco companies cooperated in the hours reduction and wage increase part, spurred like all industry not only by a desire to do their part, but also by the

---

31. *Ibid.*, p. 286.

32. *Ibid.*, quoting various U. S. Women's Bureau bulletins.

stirrings of organized labor which also had been promised new rights by the NRA.

Expanded employment was yet another matter, for to increase labor costs and at the same time to raise employment certainly is at variance with the economic facts of life. As a result of the increased labor costs, hand stemming no longer was economical for the major companies. Studies by the U. S. Bureau of Labor Statistics and by the U. S. Women's Bureau found that hours in manufacturers' stemmeries declined from 50 or 55 to 40 between 1933 and 1935, and that wages rose substantially, from an average of 19.4 cents in March 1933 to 32.5 cents two years later.[33] Faced with rising wages, the tobacco companies rushed to install stemming machines and to commence a mechanization program which continued for at least two decades, and which within a few years halved employment in many manufacturers' stemmeries.

Impact of the Fair Labor Standards Act

The independent stemmeries escaped coverage by the NRA, but the impact of minimum wages on their activities was soon felt. In 1938, Congress enacted the Fair Labor Standards Act which set the minimum wage for covered employment at 25 cents per hour. After successive amendments over the years, the minimum now stands at $1.60. The imposition of each new minimum has affected the wage policies and employment practices of the independent stemmeries, with the original 25 cent minimum having had a drastic effect.

In 1937, a study by the U. S. Bureau of Labor Statistics reported:

Negro workers in independent or dealers' tobacco stemmeries, who comprise virtually the entire working force in these establishments, are among the lowest paid employees in the country. In September 1935, the average earnings of these workers amounted to 16 cents per hour. With an average of 43.4 hours of employment per week, their weekly earnings average $6.92.

The independent stemmeries were never subject to code regulations under the National Recovery Administration . . . their earnings were much smaller and their hours longer than those of corresponding

33. "Earnings in Cigarettes, Snuff and Chewing and Smoking Tobacco Plants," *Monthly Labor Review*, Vol. XLII (May 1936), p. 1331. See also Caroline Manning, *Hours and Earnings in Tobacco Stemmeries*, Bulletin No. 127, U. S. Women's Bureau (Washington: Government Printing Office, 1936).

workers in the manufacturers' stemmeries . . . [which] are far more important in the industry than are the independent stemmeries.[34]

In a study conducted during the period from August 1940 to February 1941, the Bureau of Labor Statistics found that average hourly earnings of the employees of independent stemmeries had risen to 34.3 cents.[35]

A comparison of the average hourly and weekly earnings of Negro workers employed in 11 identical establishments in 1935 and 1940 indicates that in this 5-year period earnings almost doubled. The increase in earnings has been accompanied by a marked increase in the mechanization of stemming operators. . . .
The advent of minimum hourly earnings under the Fair Labor Standards Act has had important repercussions in the industry. . . . In 1935, for illustration, the Bureau of Labor Statistics secured wage data from a group of stemmeries, 10 of which employed no machine stemmers. In 1940-41 the identical 10 plants reported that 54 of their stemmery employees were employed on automatic stemming machines.[36]

In some of the largest stemmery establishments, employment increased, but overall it declined as many smaller ones went out of business or drastically curtailed employment. The impact of the NRA on manufacturers' stemmery employment and of the Fair Labor Standards Act on that of independent stemmeries is noted in the census data set forth in Table 10, which compares the percentage of laborers and operatives by race, 1930 and 1940, for the three key tobacco manufacturing states.

In Virginia and North Carolina, Negroes retained a majority of the laborer and operative jobs during this decade, but they were disproportionately affected by the declining employment in the industry. In Kentucky, total employment in the decade fell by approximately 2,000; Negro employment declined by *2,500*. In other words, white employment increased while Negro employment fell so the proportion of Negro laborers and operators in the state declined from 50.4 percent to 18.4 percent. The reasons for this drastic drop in Negro employment appears to be the decline in the number of stemmeries and the decline in stemmery employment in the state while one plant employing an all-white labor force expanded. In the three states, the propor-

---

34. Jacob Perlman, "Earnings and Hours of Negro Workers in Independent Tobacco Stemmeries in 1933 and 1935," *Monthly Labor Review*, Vol. XLIV (May 1937), p. 1153.

35. "Hours and Earnings of Employees of Independent Leaf-Tobacco Dealers," *Monthly Labor Review*, Vol. LIII (July 1941), p. 215.

36. *Ibid.*, pp. 215-216.

TABLE 10.   *Tobacco Industry*
Laborer and Operative Employment by Race
Major Tobacco Manufacturing States, 1930 and 1940

	1930			1940		
	Total	Negro	Percent Negro	Total	Negro	Percent Negro
Kentucky	7,006	3,534	50.4	5,052	932	18.4
North Carolina	19,756	15,049	76.2	17,078	11,063	64.8
Virginia	11,104	7,142	64.3	11,049	6,169	55.8
Total	37,866	25,725	67.9	33,179	18,164	54.7

Source: *U. S. Census of Population:*

      1930:   Vol. IV, *Occupations*, Table 11.
      1940:   Vol. III, *The Labor Force*, Parts 3, 4, and 5, Table 20.

tion of Negro laborers and operatives declined in the 1940's from 67.9 percent to 54.7 percent.

In terms of total tobacco industry employees (rather than only laborers and operatives), only North Carolina showed a majority of Negroes by 1940, and for the first time the proportion of Negro employment in the three key states dropped below 50 percent, being 45.8 percent in 1940 (Table 11) and compared with 58.7 in 1930. The jobs already open to Negroes in the industry were yielding to mechanization but no new jobs were being opened to them.

From World War II to 1960

During World War II the racial pattern in the industry was not basically changed. One company—R. J. Reynolds in Winston-Salem—upgraded a few Negroes to operative jobs on cigarette machines following the war, but generally otherwise the status quo was maintaind insofar as the racial-occupational employment pattern was concerned. Moreover, the trend of employment was up in the nearly all white cigarette manufacturing sector, but down in stemming and redrying, which has a nearly all black work force, and down in smoking, chewing, and snuff in which a sizeable proportion of the employees has always been Negro.

The declining employment in stemmeries came as a result of further mechanization. This involved not only improvement in existing equipment, but the development of new machinery, in particular a tipping and threshing machine. According to Professor Donald Dewey, who studied employment in sixteen tobacco plants in 1950-1951, this was the prime cause of the decline in Negro employment in the period around 1950.[37] In addition, the investment required to install modern stemming equipment has been beyond the means of most independents. Probably a majority of these concerns had gone out of business by 1960 and the larger ones had consolidated their operations in a few establishments. No longer do seasonal stemmeries dot the landscape in the tobacco growing states. Table 11 shows that in 1950, even North Carolina had for the first time a less than 50 percent black labor force in tobacco. Kentucky slightly reversed the downward Negro trend in the industry as Negroes gained back just a few of the jobs lost in the previous decade. In the three states, the proportion of Negro employment in the industry declined from 45.8 percent in 1940 to 37.2 percent ten years later.

The 1960's saw the declining trend of Negro employment in the industry continued despite small beginnings of a break in the racial-occupational segregation pattern. We have already noted that the R. J. Reynolds Company placed a few Negroes on cigarette machines following World War II. In 1951, Dewey reports, 6 percent of that company's cigarette machine operators were black,[38] certainly the largest Negro representation in the industry at that time and undoubtedly the first in such jobs.

Then in the mid-1950's, under pressure by the President's Committee on Government Contracts (known as the "Nixon Committee" because it was chaired by the then Vice-President), which handled equal employment issues under government contracts during the Eisenhower Administration, both Liggett & Myers and American Tobacco negotiated with locals of the Tobacco Workers International Union, then organized on a segregated basis,[39] to open up a few formerly all-white jobs to Negroes. Both companies won agreement from white locals to upgrade a limited number of Negroes—about 25 by Liggett &

---

37. Donald Dewey "Negro Employment in Sixteen Tobacco Plants," in *Selected Studies of Negro Employment in the South,* Report No. 6, NPA Committee of the South (Washington: National Planning Association, 1955), pp. 177-178.

38. *Ibid.,* pp. 170-171. Dewey does not mention Reynolds by name, but refers to a nonunion company. Only Reynolds fits this description.

39. See the ensuing section of this chapter for a discussion of TWIU policies.

TABLE 11. *Tobacco Industry*
Total and Negro Employment
Major Tobacco Manufacturing States, 1940-1960

	1940			1950			1960		
	Total	Negro	Percent Negro	Total	Negro	Percent Negro	Total	Negro	Percent Negro[a]
Kentucky	7,172	1,015	14.2	7,457	1,328	17.8	9,342	1,298	13.9
North Carolina	21,489	11,797	54.9	22,251	9,407	42.3	27,465	8,666	31.6
Virginia	13,799	6,626	48.0	10,955	4,384	40.0	12,103	3,166	26.2
Total	42,460	19,438	45.8	40,663	15,119	37.2	48,910	13,130	26.8

Source: *U. S. Census of Population:*

1940: Vol. III, *The Labor Force,* Parts 3, 4, and 5, Table 18.
1950: Vol. II, *Characteristics of the Population,* Table 83.
1960: PC(1) D, *Detailed Characteristics,* State Volumes, Table 129.

[a] For estimate basis and probable overstatement of Negro ratio, see Appendix A.

Myers in Durham and 50 by American Tobacco in Richmond. Both these concerns (and most others in the industry) had few openings to which displaced Negroes could be transferred, even if they had desired to breech the racial segregation pattern further. Continued mechanization in cigarette manufacturing and loss of market position kept job levels relatively constant for these concerns.

Few other changes were made in the racial-occupational employment pattern. P. Lorillard opened its highly automated factory in Greensboro in 1956 with only about 10 percent of the approximately 1,000 jobs going to Negroes. Continued automation increased the demand for professional and technical employees, and craftsmen, but reduced the need for unskilled labor. Although employment in cigarette manufacturing increased by about one-third between 1950 and 1960 (Table 6, p. 14), Negroes enjoyed none of the fruits of this increase for several reasons. First, the introduction and improvement of a variety of material handling devices in cigarette factories reduced the already small Negro complement in these plants. Second, in manufactured tobacco plants, where Negroes have traditionally enjoyed a much larger share of the work, declining product demand and mechanization cut the work force by about 50 percent. In addition, mechanization continued to reduce the need for unskilled labor in the stemmery departments where Negroes have traditionally been employd. Finally, in two companies where a small dent in the racial-occupational employment pattern had been made, Liggett & Myers and American, layoffs were occurring and few if any new employees were hired between 1953 and 1960.

The extent of Negro job loss in the tobacco industry during the 1950's must be estimated from the Census of Population because, for reasons that surely defy explanation, tobacco employment by race in North Carolina, Virginia, and Kentucky was not computed; instead, it was combined with two leather categories in "all other non-durable goods." [40] Even by assuming that *all* Negroes in this catch-all category worked in tobacco plants, the proportion of Negroes shows a substantial decline. Thus, for the three states combined, the decline in Negro employment would be 13.2 percent while total tobacco employment increased 20.3 percent. Table 12 shows the percentage changes for the three states, assuming again that none of the 2,264

40. See Appendix A for details of the estimate and its probable understatement of Negro job losses.

TABLE 12. *Tobacco Industry*
Percentage Increase in Total and Decrease in Negro Employment
Major Tobacco Manufacturing States, 1950-1960

	All Employees		Actual Percent Increase	Negro Employees [a]		Minimum Percent Decrease
	1950	1960	1950-1960	1950	1960	1950-1960
Kentucky	7,457	9,342	25.3	1,328	1,298	2.3
North Carolina	22,251	27,465	23.4	9,407	8,666	7.9
Virginia	10,955	12,103	10.5	4,384	3,166	27.8
Total	40,663	48,910	20.3	15,119	13,130	13.2

Source: Table 11.

[a] Negro employment in 1960 is estimated by assuming that *all* Negroes reported in the "All other non-durable goods" category worked in tobacco plants. This probably overstates Negro employment in 1960 and understates the percentage decrease during the decade. See Appendix A.

leather workers were black. Hence the decline shown for the Negor labor force is the absolute minimum and actually could have been substantially more, as explained in Appendix A.

Thus Negroes who had monopolized employment in the tobacco industry from colonial times to the latter part of the nineteenth century, and who from the nineteenth century to 1932 held a clear majority of this industry's jobs, found in 1960 that they possessed only one-fourth the employment therein as their share. A rigid racial-occupational employment pattern, only slightly dented by 1960, discriminatory hiring and employment policies, changing product demand, and the uneven impact of technological progress had all combined to work against Negroes, particularly since 1932. To this must be added union policies which, as shall be documented below, served to institutionalize the difficulties of Negro members, rather than to work to overcome them.

THE IMPACT OF UNIONISM TO 1960

Unionism in tobacco manufacturing existed only on the fringes of the industry before the 1930's. The Tobacco Workers' International Union, unable to dent the antiunion policies of the tobacco "trust" or the four major successor companies, American, Liggett & Myers, Lorillard, and Reynolds, bought recognition from some smaller companies in exchange for granting these companies the right to use the union label.[41] With management in effect unionizing its employees to obtain the label in small companies and with the TWIU unable to penetrate the bulk of the industry, unionism probably had no impact on employer racial policies prior to World War I.

During World War I, membership in the TWIU tripled to 15,000, largely as a result of winning recognition from R. J. Reynolds in Winston-Salem. Negro organizers had been used with excellent results. Following the war, however, Reynolds reduced wages without consulting the union, which offered no overt resistance. After membership declined to 1,500 in 1925, the TWIU decided to attempt to unionize Reynolds a second time. Some 7,000 employees were enrolled, but when Reynolds refused to recognize the union, it again took no overt action to redeem its campaign promises. The resultant distrust of the TWIU by Reynolds employees, and apparently especially the feeling on the part of Negro employees that they had been victimized in the two unionization attempts, has plagued TWIU's efforts to organize Reynolds ever since.

In December 1933, the unionization of three Brown & Williamson plants by a union label sale touched off a revolt within the union. The revolt was led by workers who received just about enough in wage increases to pay the compulsory union dues. The leader of the TWIU since its founding in 1895 was deposed, and the TWIU was converted from a label-selling organization into a typical business union. Meanwhile, the bulk of the industry, except for Reynolds, was unionized.

Most of the TWIU locals in the South were organized on a separate racial-local basis prior to 1946. This method of organizing was, of course, facilitated by the racial-occupational segregation pattern in the industry. The Negro locals had full rights as locals, and usually negotiated on a joint basis with the white locals. At Liggett & Myers Durham plants, for example, there was one white local having jurisdiction over most employees in the cigarette operations, a Negro local with jurisdiction over Negro employees attached to these operations, and a second Negro local with jurisdiction over stemming, storage, and blend-

---

41. The history of the TWIU prior to 1942 is based on Herbert R. Northrup, "The Tobacco Workers International Union," *Quarterly Journal of Economics*, Vol. LVI (August 1942), pp. 606-626; and Northrup, *Organized Labor and the Negro, op. cit.*, Chapter IV.

ing plant employees. These three locals, together with the one Negro and one white local in the same company's Richmond plant, negotiated a joint contract with Liggett & Myers. Likewise, three white and three Negro locals representing employees at American's Durham, Reedsville, and Richmond plants negotiated jointly.

By running their segregated locals, the Negro tobacco workers developed leadership and were insured a voice at national union meetings as well as representation on local or company-wide bargaining sessions. Negroes also have played a role in the national leadership. Negro representatives served on the national executive board of the TWIU between 1897 and 1900. Then after a forty-year hiatus, George Benjamin, a Negro, was elected a vice-president. He retained that post until he retired in 1968 and was succeeded by Oliver Shaw, who is also black. A second vice-presidency has been held by a Negro since 1944, and other Negroes have served as organizers, committeemen, local presidents, etc.

Despite some advantages of the separate local system and despite efforts of the TWIU leadership to represent their Negro membership, the separate local system had definite disadvantages for Negroes. It institutionalized the status quo, adding another barrier which maintained the racial-occupational segregation pattern, and did so in a period when Negroes were disproportionately losing jobs to mechanization. Moreover, in some instances, separate locals prevented Negroes, who initially comprised a majority of a company's employees, from controlling a local bargaining situation.

The separate local system also maintained racial exclusiveness by providing contacts only for local leaders. In some areas, such as Durham, there was good cooperation among Negro and white leadership. In Richmond, however, the union movement affiliated with the American Federation of Labor was at first quite antagonistic to Negroes. The Central Labor Union denied TWIU locals affiliation in the 1930's, but the white TWIU locals were able to join it. TWIU leaders in this area largely ignored Negroes, attempting for a time to organize only whites. This opened the way for a challenge by a rival union.

Rival Unionism in Tobacco

Employees of independent stemmeries, like most seasonal workers, are difficult and expensive to organize. The labor force of a facility can vary from year to year and employees are easily replaceable. Hence the TWIU at first did not exert a major effort to unionize these employees. In 1937 in Richmond, however, a strike at two independent stemmeries was given leadership by the Southern Negro Youth Congress "controlled by the Communist Party." [42] Union recognition was secured and three other contracts obtained. These locals then affiliated with what was then called the United Cannery, Agricultural and Allied Workers of America, a CIO affiliate which later changed its name to the Food, Tobacco and Allied Workers (FTA). This union, which sedulously adhered to the Communist Party line throughout its life, employed the Southern Negro Youth Congress personnel as organizers and began a drive to enroll tobacco workers in Richmond. Its support came largely from Negroes, in contrast to the white-employee oriented TWIU leadership in Richmond. The TWIU emerged victorious in National Labor Relations Board representation elections in Richmond plants, leaving the CIO affiliate only its stemmery locals, which in time also apparently became extinct.[43]

It was in Winston-Salem, however, that the FTA scored its greatest victory, winning a NLRB election in 1944. Unquestionably, as before, its support came principally from Negroes. The TWIU withdrew from the election contest after an earlier indecisive election showed it to have an insufficient following, but again one that was much stronger among whites than Negroes.[44]

The FTA's success was short lived. In 1948, it lost bargaining rights following a long strike. The FTA's position among employees had been materially weakened by its leaders' refusal to sign the non-Communist affidavits required by the Taft-Hartley Act of 1947,[45] and by their militant concern with, and adherence to, Communist Party policies, such as foreign policy issues, at

---

42. F. Ray Marshall, *Labor in the South* (Cambridge: Harvard University Press, 1967), p. 217.

43. These locals seem to have lasted through World War II, but apparently disappeared as unions when, as explained below, the parent union also disintegrated. This has been the fate of most stemmery locals. The TWIU now has 24 locals in 19 independent stemmeries, but between 1945 and 1969, it chartered 87 locals, most in independent stemmeries, most of which are no longer in existence. (Interview, Washington, D.C., December 3, 1969.)

44. Northrup, *Organized Labor and the Negro*, *op. cit.*, pp. 115-117.

45. This requirement was altered by the Landrum-Griffin Act of 1959.

the expense of local collective bargaining problems.[46] Soon after this strike, the FTA, along with several other unions, was expelled from the CIO on charges of Communist domination. Afterwards it completely disintegrated.[47]

The TWIU, the FTA, and the United Transport Service Employees (then a CIO union led by and comprising mainly porters at railroad stations), attempted to organize Reynolds employees in 1950. Since the employees were split both on racial lines and on union adherence, and since unionism had left a bad taste of strife and failure for Reynolds employees since World War I, the attempt was a failure.[48] As a result, Reynolds remains today a nonunion concern, a fact which has had an important effect on its ability to move away from the racial-occupational job pattern during the 1960's.

Impact of Rival Unionism

The departure of effective rival unionism left the field to the TWIU. Unfortunately for Negroes, the union which had promised, and indeed practiced, equalitarian policy beyond that of the TWIU had been decisively handicapped by ideological subservience to extraneous policies, and therefore could have little direct impact. Undoubtedly, however, the FTA did force the TWIU to liberalize its policies. As already noted, the FTA presence forced the TWIU to concern itself effectively with the Negro tobacco employees of Richmond. And in 1946, following the loss of Reynolds employees to the FTA, the TWIU resolved not to organize any local plants on a segregated basis.

In 1956, when Lorillard moved its operation from Jersey City, New Jersey, to Greensboro, North Carolina, the TWIU organized the plant on a single local basis. Only 10 percent of the

---

46. Based on interviews, review of FTA papers, etc.

47. The FTA and another Communist-led organization affiliated with Local 65, which had disaffiliated from Retail, Wholesale and Department Store Employees, CIO. Local 65 later broke with the Communists, and returned to the CIO. In 1969, it disaffiliated again, this time from the AFL-CIO to join the Alliance for Labor Action. Most FTA locals which survived, however, left FTA and joined other unions. See F. S. O'Brien, "The 'Communist Dominated' Unions in the United States Since 1950," *Labor History*, Vol. IX (Spring 1968), especially pp. 189-193.

48. F. Ray Marshall, *The Negro and Organized Labor* (New York: John Wiley & Sons, 1965), p. 189. In this book, Professor Marshall correctly places the year of the FTA's last strike at Reynolds as 1948. His *Labor in the South, op. cit.*, p. 217, incorrectly refers to the year as 1946.

employees hired at Lorillard's highly automated plant were Negroes, however, and they found that their integrated local had
few advantages. The company and union negotiated a contract
with strict departmental seniority which was a carryover from
the Jersey City plants. With Lorillard adhering to the traditional
racial-occupational segregation pattern in its hiring policies, Negroes found that they were as rigidly confined to traditional jobs
(the few that remained) as they were in older plants where
segregated locals prevailed. For under departmental seniority,
no one had promotion or layoff rights except in his department
or job grouping.

Craft Unions in Tobacco Plants

An additional barrier to Negro upward mobility in tobacco
plants was erected in the early days of unionism. A number of
craft unions, especially the International Brotherhood of Electri-
cal Workers, the International Association of Machinists, and
others varying from plant to plant, won bargaining rights for
craftsmen. These unions were traditionally antagonistic to Negro employment and upgrading and therefore tended to reinforce the racial-occupational segregation pattern.[49] Negroes de-
siring opportunities to transfer to craftsmen jobs or to train as
apprentices in plants so unionized in the tobacco industry, as in
other industries, would have encountered the organized hostility
of these unions and their members in addition to the other difficulties traditionally inherent in the tobacco industry's employment patterns and policies.

In Louisville, the Teamsters' Union organized the stemmery of
American Tobacco, while the TWIU organized the manufacturing facility. This gave Negroes no rights in the latter and added
an additional union barrier to Negro upgrading. The abandon-
ment of those operations by American in 1970 came before this
interunion issue was resolved.

Union Impact on Racial Policies Prior to 1960—Final Comment

A study of the tobacco industry's racial policies in the 1950's,
which noted that the proportion of Negro employment had steadily declined, contained this contradictory paragraph:

---

49. For analysis of craft union policies in this era, see Northrup, *Organized
Labor and the Negro, op. cit.*, Chapters I-II.

Nevertheless, in view of the large number of other circumstances that affect (or in the absence of union organization could affect) the conditions of Negro employment in the industry, one cannot fairly assert that the union policy of segregation has adversely affected the interest of its Negro members. In established plants, union policy discourages, if it does not preclude the upgrading of Negro workers; in the event of falling employment, it would block the transfer of Negro jobs to white workers. As yet, the tobacco firms probably have a free hand in staffing new plants.[50]

One must agree that employers have prime responsibility for the racial-occupational segregation pattern in the industry, and they indeed do the hiring with a free hand. Moreover, the proportion of Negroes declined in the nonunion, as well as the union labor force from 1932 to 1960. The TWIU completely acquiesced to maintaining the pattern of employment and therefore represented its white members well to the detriment of, and at the expense of, its Negro members. New white workers were employed while black TWIU members were laid off with little or no union opposition. Even token integration in the 1950's was initiated by the companies under government pressure, with the union, which could exert little control over its local affiliates, merely acquiescing. Integration at nonunion Reynolds, though token, was ahead of unionized plants. Surely it is not possible to equate union protection against layoffs with lack of opportunity for transfers and promotions in a situation in which the brunt of the layoffs was borne by Negroes while cigarette employment was expanding in jobs open almost exclusively to whites.

To repeat, the prime responsibility for the disadvantaged position of Negro tobacco workers and their steadily worsening proportion of job opportunities rested with the tobacco companies. The TWIU, and particularly its local unions and its dominant white membership, aided in the enforcement of the racial-occupational segregation pattern and seemed to institutionalize and support the denial of jobs to black union members even when these members were being laid off and new white workers hired.

---

50. Dewey, *op. cit.*, p. 177.

CHAPTER IV

The 1960's — Attempting to End Segregation

The racial-occupational segregation pattern in tobacco manufacturing, which endured for nearly a century after the mechanization of cigarette manufacturing, finally began to crumble in the 1960's under the impetus of governmental intervention and civil rights legislation. By then, however, the proportion of Negroes in the industry was the lowest since colonial times. This chapter discusses developments in the decade of the 1960's and analyzes the changes which have occurred since the 1960 Census of Population.

QUALITATIVE IMPROVEMENT, QUANTITATIVE STABILITY

In the 1950's the efforts of the President's Committee on Government Contracts (Nixon Committee) resulted in a few small dents in the racial-occupational segregation pattern, and even earlier, R. J. Reynolds Company had moved some Negroes into traditionally all-white jobs. Then when the Kennedy Administration created the President's Committee on Equal Employment Opportunity (PCEEO) to replace the Nixon Committee and gave the newer committee stronger authority, complaints poured in from nearly every major tobacco facility. By the time Title VII of the Civil Rights Act became effective in July 1965, changes were well underway.

Despite the favorable qualitative developments of the 1960's, our data show little or no quantitative improvement in the Negro employment ratio. Continued mechanization and automation and the linkage of smoking and health problems with consequent decline in domestic tobacco consumption have precluded employment expansion. Moreover, during the first few years of the decade, Negroes continued to be barred from most traditionally white departments and were disproportionately affected by the continued technological and productivity improvements as they had been since the early 1930's.

The initial government response under PCEEO to charges of discrimination in the tobacco industry was to pressure the companies to open up all departments to all races and to pressure the TWIU and the companies to abolish separate racial-locals and bargaining arrangements. The response of the companies to the former was to tack the Negro seniority list on the bottom of former white jobs, and vice-versa. Since few openings occurred, there was little upward movement, and the complaints of Negro employees to the government continued. Meanwhile, Reynolds opened a new plant in Winston-Salem on a fully integrated basis and then moved to desegregate its older facilities; in other companies the Negro local unions were merged into the white locals, and later new seniority arrangements were either worked out or litigated. The details and problems involved in these changes vary among companies and are discussed later in this chapter, following an analysis of the basic statistics for the period.

The 1966 Equal Employment Opportunity Commission Data

Data by race, collected from employers of 100 or more, have been published by the Equal Employment Opportunity Commission for 1966. In the three key tobacco manufacturing states, these data show that 25.6 percent of all employees in 71 tobacco plants were Negro (Table 13). As noted in previous studies, EEOC data are not strictly comparable to those of the Census of Population. The exclusion of plants which have less than 100 employees from EEOC coverage could eliminate some small stemmeries which have an all-Negro labor force and which were included in census data. More significant, of course, is that census data are based on responses by people to interrogators, while EEOC reports are filed by employers from payroll figures. On the other hand, both the census and the EEOC data for the three states do include the few cigar employees working there.

A further complication is the failure of the census to report tobacco employees by race for the three key states since 1950. Table 11 (p. 31) therefore estimated the maximum percentage of Negroes in 1960 as 26.8 of the total employment. Remarkably, Table 13 shows that percentage to be 25.6 percent in 1966. In fact, these figures support the author's impressions, based upon field interviews, that the precipitous decline in the ratio of Negro tobacco employment, which began with the NRA minimum wage codes in the early 1930's, had been slowed, or possibly halted, by 1966.

TABLE 13. *Tobacco Industry*
Employment by Race, Sex, and Occupational Group
Kentucky, North Carolina, and Virginia, 1966

Occupational Group	All Employees			Male			Female		
	Total	Negro	Percent Negro	Total	Negro	Percent Negro	Total	Negro	Percent Negro
Officials and managers	3,688	42	1.1	3,583	42	1.2	105	—	—
Professionals	872	8	0.9	825	6	0.7	47	2	4.3
Technicians	1,103	31	2.8	855	27	3.2	248	4	1.6
Sales workers	2,025	44	2.2	1,951	42	2.2	74	2	2.7
Office and clerical	3,352	166	5.0	1,267	57	4.5	2,085	109	5.2
Total white collar	11,040	291	2.6	8,481	174	2.1	2,559	117	4.6
Craftsmen	4,963	137	2.8	4,835	129	2.7	128	8	6.2
Operatives	19,716	3,183	15.9	11,022	2,473	22.4	8,694	660	7.6
Laborers	18,792	9,572	50.9	10,843	6,298	58.1	7,949	3,274	41.2
Service workers	2,070	1,353	65.4	1,618	1,012	62.5	452	341	75.4
Total blue collar	45,541	14,195	31.2	28,318	9,912	35.0	17,223	4,283	24.9
Total	56,581	14,486	25.6	36,799	10,086	27.4	19,782	4,400	22.2

Source: U. S. Equal Employment Opportunity Commission, *Job Patterns for Minorities and Women in Private Industry,* Report No. 1 (Washington: Government Printing Office, 1966), Part II.

Tables 14-16 show the same EEOC data for the three states individually. Comparing again (with due regard for the limitations of such comparisons) the data in these tables with those in Table 11, we find that both North Carolina and Virginia show similar percentages in both years—the former down 2.6 percentage points in 1966, the latter up 1.8. Kentucky is up 4.1 percentage points in 1966 over 1960, apparently as a result of a large increase in stemmery operations reporting there.

The 1964-1968 Field Sample

The EEOC data reported in Tables 13-16 are based on the period immediately after the 1965 effective date of Title VII of the Civil Rights Act of 1964 and therefore, as noted in other studies in this Series, do not reflect significant later developments. Accordingly, as was done for other studies, data were gathered for the three years 1964, 1966, and 1968. Although these data include most establishments of all major concerns, they do not, unlike those of the EEOC or Census of Population, include any independent stemmeries or the few cigar facilities in the three key states. Thus the sample data for 1966 report 47,382 employees as compared with 56,581 in the EEOC data of the same year (Tables 13 and 18).

Given the dissimilarities in coverage, and especially the absence of the nearly all black independent stemmery labor force from the author's sample, it is not surprising that the percentage of Negroes for 1966 shown in Table 18 is only 21.8 as compared with 25.6 in Table 13. It should be borne in mind, therefore, that by reason of the exclusion of data for independent stemmeries from the author's sample, the number and ratio of Negro employees for 1964, 1966, and 1968 are understated. On the other hand, the occupational analysis which follows is enhanced by comparing the trend over the three years.

OCCUPATIONAL CHANGE, 1964-1968

Historically Negroes have occupied few jobs above that of operative in the tobacco industry, and have been heavily concentrated in the lowest skill jobs—laborers and service workers. By 1960 there had been very little change. A few Negroes had been employed for special sales work—largely sales promotion among members of their own race—and some Negroes were employed as supervisors in stemmeries, but the concentration of blacks in the lowest level jobs remained.

TABLE 14. *Tobacco Industry*
Employment by Race, Sex, and Occupational Group
Kentucky, 1966

Occupational Group	All Employees			Male			Female		
	Total	Negro	Percent Negro	Total	Negro	Percent Negro	Total	Negro	Percent Negro
Officials and managers	902	8	0.9	877	8	0.9	25	—	—
Professionals	132	1	0.8	126	—	—	6	1	16.7
Technicians	217	3	1.4	131	2	1.5	86	1	1.2
Sales workers	610	17	2.8	610	17	2.8	—	—	—
Office and clerical	1,025	28	2.7	378	8	2.1	647	20	3.1
Total white collar	2,886	57	2.0	2,122	35	1.6	764	22	2.9
Craftsmen	983	32	3.3	964	32	3.3	19	—	—
Operatives	5,253	547	10.4	2,524	434	17.2	2,729	113	4.1
Laborers	6,645	2,108	31.7	4,212	1,336	31.7	2,433	772	31.7
Service workers	487	179	36.8	329	118	35.9	158	61	38.6
Total blue collar	13,368	2,866	21.4	8,029	1,920	23.9	5,339	946	17.7
Total	16,254	2,923	18.0	10,151	1,955	19.3	6,103	968	15.9

Source: U. S. Equal Employment Opportunity Commission, *Job Patterns for Minorities and Women in Private Industry,* Report No. 1 (Washington: Government Printing Office, 1966), Part II.

TABLE 15. *Tobacco Industry*
Employment by Race, Sex, and Occupational Group
North Carolina, 1966

Occupational Group	All Employees			Male			Female		
	Total	Negro	Percent Negro	Total	Negro	Percent Negro	Total	Negro	Percent Negro
Officials and managers	1,922	14	0.7	1,917	14	0.7	5	—	—
Professionals	452	3	0.7	438	2	0.5	14	1	7.1
Technicians	644	23	3.6	579	21	3.6	65	2	3.1
Sales workers	1,407	26	1.8	1,333	24	1.8	74	2	2.7
Office and clerical	1,707	100	5.9	643	29	4.5	1,064	71	6.7
Total white collar	6,132	166	2.7	4,910	90	1.8	1,222	76	6.2
Craftsmen	2,933	85	2.9	2,824	77	2.7	109	8	7.3
Operatives	9,204	1,603	17.4	6,033	1,340	22.2	3,171	263	8.3
Laborers	8,302	5,295	63.8	4,352	3,472	79.8	3,950	1,823	46.2
Service workers	1,156	880	76.1	919	655	71.3	237	225	94.9
Total blue collar	21,595	7,863	36.4	14,128	5,544	39.2	7,467	2,319	31.1
Total	27,727	8,029	29.0	19,038	5,634	29.6	8,689	2,395	27.6

Source: U. S. Equal Employment Opportunity Commission, *Job Patterns for Minorities and Women in Private Industry*, Report No. 1 (Washington: Government Printing Office, 1966), Part II.

TABLE 16. Tobacco Industry
Employment by Race, Sex, and Occupational Group
Virginia, 1966

Occupational Group	All Employees			Male			Female		
	Total	Negro	Percent Negro	Total	Negro	Percent Negro	Total	Negro	Percent Negro
Officials and managers	864	20	2.3	789	20	2.5	75	—	—
Professionals	288	4	1.4	261	4	1.5	27	—	—
Technicians	242	5	2.1	145	4	2.8	97	1	1.0
Sales workers	8	1	12.5	8	1	12.5	—	—	—
Office and clerical	620	38	6.1	246	20	8.1	374	18	4.8
Total white collar	2,022	68	3.4	1,449	49	3.4	573	19	3.3
Craftsmen	1,047	20	1.9	1,047	20	1.9	—	—	—
Operatives	5,259	983	18.7	2,465	699	28.4	2,794	284	10.2
Laborers	3,845	2,169	56.4	2,279	1,490	65.4	1,566	679	43.4
Service workers	427	294	68.9	370	239	64.6	57	55	96.5
Total blue collar	10,578	3,466	32.8	6,161	2,448	39.7	4,417	1,018	23.0
Total	12,600	3,534	28.0	7,610	2,497	32.8	4,990	1,037	20.8

Source: U. S. Equal Employment Opportunity Commission, *Job Patterns for Minorities and Women in Private Industry*, Report No. 1 (Washington: Government Printing Office, 1966), Part II.

Tables 17-19 show, with one minor exception, that the occupational representation of Negroes improved in the 1964-1968 period. In each of the white collar classifications, the ratio of Negroes rose between 1964 and 1968, except for professionals, where a minute rise in 1966 was cancelled out in 1968. Likewise, the proportion of Negroes in the craftsman and operative classifications increased over this four-year period. On the other hand, the proportion of Negroes working as laborers declined slightly, and those employed as service workers declined substantially. This would indicate both upgrading of Negroes and employment of whites for once all-Negro jobs.

White Collar Jobs in the Three Southern States

In the three states, the total number of salaried positions in 1968 was only 10,140, of which Negroes held 279. Thus small increases in Negro representation result in relatively large percentage changes—101 additional Negro salaried employees resulted in an increase in the ratio from 1.8 to 2.8 percent. In view of the fact that white collar personnel of most companies are likely to be in New York offices instead of southern factories, these data also understate such Negro representation as does exist. This should be borne in mind in the subsequent discussion.

In the officials and managers group, the number of Negroes more than doubled—from 25 to 64. Most of these are, to be sure, first line supervisors and a sizable number are in the processing departments where the labor force is all or nearly all black. There have, however, been some higher rated appointments, including several in personnel departments.

Professionals and technical employees are not numerous in the industry, which now finds attracting blacks very difficult. Qualified Negro professionals and technical personnel have numerous opportunities for good jobs. The tobacco industry has neither glamor nor an historical record of fair employment. Moreover, its southern location is frequently considered "out of bounds" for northern-born Negroes who often do not want to chance the environment there. While the number of Negro professional employees has remained about the same, the number of technicians has increased from 18 in 1964 to 34 in 1968, 3.0 percent of all technical employees.

TABLE 17. Tobacco Industry
Employment by Race, Sex, and Occupational Group
6 Companies
Kentucky, North Carolina, and Virginia, 1964

Occupational Group	All Employees			Male			Female		
	Total	Negro	Percent Negro	Total	Negro	Percent Negro	Total	Negro	Percent Negro
Officials and managers	2,806	25	0.9	2,798	25	0.9	8	—	—
Professionals	828	6	0.7	782	4	0.5	46	2	4.3
Technicians	1,170	18	1.5	928	13	1.4	242	5	2.1
Sales workers	1,917	38	2.0	1,870	38	2.0	47	—	—
Office and clerical	3,305	91	2.8	1,280	40	3.1	2,025	51	2.5
Total white collar	10,026	178	1.8	7,658	120	1.6	2,368	58	2.4
Craftsmen	4,950	82	1.7	4,760	82	1.7	190	—	—
Operatives	18,072	2,368	13.1	10,139	1,783	17.6	7,933	585	7.4
Laborers	12,385	5,926	47.8	7,128	4,536	63.6	5,257	1,390	26.4
Service workers	1,993	1,355	68.0	1,608	1,069	66.5	385	286	74.3
Total blue collar	37,400	9,731	26.0	23,635	7,470	31.6	13,765	2,261	16.4
Total	47,426	9,909	20.9	31,293	7,590	24.3	16,183	2,319	14.4

Source: Data in the author's possession.

TABLE 18. *Tobacco Industry*
Employment by Race, Sex, and Occupational Group
6 Companies
Kentucky, North Carolina, and Virginia, 1966

Occupational Group	All Employees			Male			Female		
	Total	Negro	Percent Negro	Total	Negro	Percent Negro	Total	Negro	Percent Negro
Officials and managers	3,021	37	1.2	2,939	37	1.3	82	—	—
Professionals	838	8	1.0	791	6	0.8	47	2	4.3
Technicians	1,040	23	2.2	802	20	2.5	238	3	1.3
Sales workers	1,986	44	2.2	1,913	42	2.2	73	2	2.7
Office and clerical	2,891	100	3.5	1,018	48	4.7	1,873	52	2.8
Total white collar	9,776	212	2.2	7,463	153	2.1	2,313	59	2.6
Craftsmen	4,542	86	1.9	4,441	86	1.9	101	—	—
Operatives	18,186	2,670	14.7	10,367	2,086	20.1	7,819	584	7.5
Laborers	12,962	6,114	47.2	7,459	4,515	60.5	5,503	1,599	29.1
Service workers	1,916	1,262	65.9	1,512	965	63.8	404	297	73.5
Total blue collar	37,606	10,132	26.9	23,779	7,652	32.2	13,827	2,480	17.9
Total	47,382	10,344	21.8	31,242	7,805	25.0	16,140	2,539	15.7

Source: Data in the author's possession.

TABLE 19. *Tobacco Industry*
Employment by Race, Sex, and Occupational Group
6 Companies
Kentucky, North Carolina, and Virginia, 1968

Occupational Group	All Employees			Male			Female		
	Total	Negro	Percent Negro	Total	Negro	Percent Negro	Total	Negro	Percent Negro
Officials and managers	3,326	64	1.9	3,247	64	2.0	79	—	—
Professionals	966	7	0.7	884	5	0.6	82	2	2.4
Technicians	1,124	34	3.0	884	29	3.3	240	5	2.1
Sales workers	1,319	41	3.1	1,272	41	3.2	47	—	—
Office and clerical	3,405	133	3.9	1,127	42	3.7	2,278	91	4.0
Total white collar	10,140	279	2.8	7,414	181	2.4	2,726	98	3.6
Craftsmen	4,841	107	2.2	4,814	107	2.2	27	—	—
Operatives	19,880	3,438	17.3	11,130	2,581	23.2	8,750	857	9.8
Laborers	13,127	6,175	47.0	8,099	4,664	57.6	5,028	1,511	30.1
Service workers	1,973	1,090	55.2	1,632	862	52.8	341	228	66.9
Total blue collar	39,821	10,810	27.1	25,675	8,214	32.0	14,146	2,596	18.4
Total	49,961	11,089	22.2	33,089	8,395	25.4	16,872	2,694	16.0

Source: Data in the author's possession.

In sales, tobacco has only a few Negroes, but it is by no means behind the general industry pattern. Tobacco companies have been utilizing Negro route salesmen and promotion men for many years, at first to increase their sales among Negroes, and more recently in general sales work and promotion. Most of these salesmen are not based in the three states. Office and clerical personnel, on the other hand, were almost all white in the three southern states, both in tobacco plants and others, prior to 1960. As in other large industries, tobacco companies are now doing extensive recruiting and training to increase their share of Negroes in these jobs.

Three State Differences

Some surprising differences are apparent when comparing field data for Kentucky, North Carolina, and Virginia, especially for total employment and for white collar jobs. Table 20 shows the percentage distributions in the three states, based upon Tables 17-19 and Appendix Tables B-1 to B-9. First, there is the relative stability of North Carolina over the four-year period, and in contrast, the jump in the Negro proportion in Kentucky and Virginia. The latter state, for the first time in this century, had a larger proportion of Negro tobacco workers than did its neighboring state just to the south.

Kentucky also saw surprising gains in the ratio of Negro employment, but most of its gains were concentrated in the lower rated jobs. Both Virginia and North Carolina Negro tobacco workers scored qualitative gains by increasing their proportion of salaried jobs and of the top two blue collar jobs. The gains in salaried positions for Negroes were especially impressive in Virginia, where the proportion of officials and managers, technicians, and office and clerical employees not only rose but substantially exceeded those groups in other states. Nor were any sales workers reported for Kentucky in 1968.

Virginia no longer boasts the headquarters of major tobacco companies, so no sales workers were recorded there. The proportion of Negro white collar employees was 2.6 percent in Kentucky, 2.4 percent in North Carolina, and 4.0 percent in Virginia. The 3.1 ratio in North Carolina for this group in effect is the industry figure for the three states and probably reflects local sales personnel of the one company headquartered there.

TABLE 20. Tobacco Industry
Percent Negro Employment by Occupational Group
Major Tobacco Manufacturing States
1964, 1966, 1968

Occupational Group	Total			Kentucky			North Carolina			Virginia		
	1964	1966	1968	1964	1966	1968	1964	1966	1968	1964	1966	1968
Officials and managers	0.9	1.2	1.9	0.8	0.9	1.8	0.6	0.8	1.3	2.4	2.5	3.4
Professionals	0.7	1.0	0.7	0.9	0.8	—	0.4	0.7	1.0	1.3	1.5	0.6
Technicians	1.5	2.2	3.0	1.1	1.6	1.4	1.8	2.5	3.3	1.0	2.1	3.6
Sales workers	2.0	2.2	3.1	2.6	2.9	—a	1.7	1.9	3.1	—a	20.0b	—a
Office and clerical	2.8	3.5	3.9	3.1	3.0	4.0	2.2	3.0	3.2	4.4	5.8	5.9
Total white collar	1.8	2.2	2.8	2.1	2.1	2.6	1.5	1.8	2.4	2.8	3.3	4.0
Craftsmen	1.7	1.9	2.2	0.8	1.0	0.6	2.1	2.3	2.8	1.0	1.4	2.1
Operatives	13.1	14.7	17.3	5.6	8.8	10.2	15.2	16.1	18.9	15.6	17.5	22.9
Laborers	47.8	47.2	47.0	22.7	30.3	27.9	54.3	54.4	53.9	52.7	50.1	55.8
Service workers	68.0	65.9	55.2	36.0	35.3	36.9	79.2	78.3	61.2	67.1	67.2	60.9
Total blue collar	26.0	26.9	27.1	11.9	17.4	16.5	30.6	30.5	29.8	27.9	28.9	33.9
Total	20.9	21.8	22.2	9.7	14.0	14.2	23.6	24.1	23.2	24.6	24.9	29.2

Source: Tables 17-19 and Appendix Tables B-1 to B-9.

a No sales personnel of either race reported.

b One Negro of a total of five.

The gains made by Negroes in Virginia tobacco plants during the 1960's are probably the result both of labor market and civil rights factors. Richmond and Petersburg, where the Virginia tobacco industry is concentrated, have both become heavily black populated cities in which Negroes are clearly close to a majority. (See Table 4, p. 11.) Richmond in particular has been in a full employment situation for the entire decade. With most tobacco factories located in heavily Negro neighborhoods, and with continued pressure for fair employment, the pressures and the needs have coincided.

In North Carolina, there is more competition for tobacco plant jobs between whites and Negroes, with at least two newer plants attracting many applicants for the available jobs. Despite the affirmative action, particularly of one, but also of other companies, the percentage of Negroes, at an all-time low in 1960, has not increased substantially since then.

Louisville, Kentucky, has attracted several major employers—International Harvester, General Electric, and DuPont, for example—which pay much higher wages than does the tobacco industry. It is quite likely that jobs have opened to Negroes in Louisville tobacco plants as whites have been attracted elsewhere. How the closing of the American plant in Louisville will affect these data remains to be seen. Since some of the work will be moved to American's three North Carolina plants, it could improve Negro employment there.

White Collar Jobs in the Total Tobacco Company Employment

For a comparison with other industries, it is appropriate to look at tobacco white collar employment, not only in the three key manufacturing states, but also in the companies as a whole, and (for the four companies which maintain them) in their New York offices. Table 21 summarizes the total occupational group breakdown by race and sex for the six major tobacco companies for 1968, and Table 22 provides the data for the New York offices of four.

As pointed out in Chapter II, the tobacco companies are more and more either becoming conglomerates or are being absorbed by such diversified concerns. Hence the data in Tables 21 and 22 include employees of non-tobacco aspects or divisions of these companies' businesses. The bulk of their employees as of 1968 were, however, directly concerned with the tobacco industry.

TABLE 21. Tobacco Industry
Employment by Race, Sex, and Occupational Group
Consolidated Report Data, 6 Companies, 1968

Occupational Group	All Employees			Male			Female		
	Total	Negro	Percent Negro	Total	Negro	Percent Negro	Total	Negro	Percent Negro
Officials and managers	4,814	91	1.9	4,691	90	1.9	123	1	0.8
Professionals	1,473	13	0.9	1,326	10	0.8	147	3	2.0
Technicians	1,456	46	3.2	1,193	34	2.8	263	12	4.6
Sales workers	5,411	195	3.6	5,325	194	3.6	86	1	1.2
Office and clerical	5,658	241	4.3	1,797	72	4.0	3,861	169	4.4
Total white collar	18,812	586	3.1	14,332	400	2.8	4,480	186	4.2
Craftsmen	6,095	144	2.4	6,008	137	2.3	87	7	8.0
Operatives	21,781	3,822	17.5	11,497	2,692	23.4	10,284	1,130	11.0
Laborers	14,560	6,600	45.3	8,786	4,916	56.0	5,774	1,684	29.2
Service workers	2,104	1,156	54.9	1,717	895	52.1	387	261	67.4
Total blue collar	44,540	11,722	26.3	28,008	8,640	30.8	16,532	3,082	18.6
Total	63,352	12,308	19.4	42,340	9,040	21.4	21,012	3,268	15.6

Source: Data in the author's possession.

TABLE 22. *Tobacco Industry*
Employment by Race, Sex, and Occupational Group
4 Companies, New York Offices, 1968

Occupational Group	All Employees			Male			Female		
	Total	Negro	Percent Negro	Total	Negro	Percent Negro	Total	Negro	Percent Negro
Officials and managers	564	5	0.9	554	5	0.9	10	—	—
Professionals	161	6	3.7	155	5	3.2	6	1	16.7
Technicians	38	3	7.9	37	3	8.1	1	—	—
Sales workers	801	29	3.6	766	28	3.7	35	1	2.9
Office and clerical	1,574	101	6.4	406	26	6.4	1,168	75	6.4
Total white collar	3,138	144	4.6	1,918	67	3.5	1,220	77	6.3
Craftsmen	10	2	20.0	8	2	25.0	2	—	—
Operatives	9	4	44.4	7	2	28.6	2	2	100.0
Laborers	—	—	—	—	—	—	—	—	—
Service workers	21	5	23.8	18	5	27.8	3	—	—
Total blue collar	40	11	27.5	33	9	27.3	7	2	28.6
Total	3,178	155	4.9	1,951	76	3.9	1,227	79	6.4

Source: Data in the author's possession.

It is apparent that Negro white collar employment is higher in all categories in the consolidated reports than in those pertaining to plants in the three key states except for the officials and managers group. This last includes supervisors who are, of course, in the plants. Total Negro white collar employment of 1968 was 3.1 percent in the consolidated reports, 2.8 percent for the three state plant compilation (Table 19). Undoubtedly, the companies' greater success in recruiting salaried personnel for the New York and other northern big city offices is a factor in this. Table 22 shows a 4.6 salaried employment figure for the New York offices, buttressed by a 6.4 percent office and clerical representation. In Virginia, the overall salaried figure for 1968 was 4.0 percent; for office and clerical, 5.9 percent (Table 20).

One can conclude this discussion of white collar employment by noting that in the South, all of the tobacco companies are attempting to recruit Negro salaried employees, and are not far behind other industry in this regard. They have had greater success in sales personnel than in professional or technical employees. In New York City, they have maintained a stance that is near average.[51]

Blue Collar Employment

As already noted, the occupational structure has improved for Negroes since 1964. The percentage of craftsmen rose from 1.7 to 2.2 (Tables 17-19); that of operatives from 13.1 to 17.3; meanwhile, Negro representation in the unskilled laborer category remained constant and that in service workers declined from 68 to 55.2 percent. Change is not rapid. Job openings are relatively few and production has recently been constant only because foreign sales have been making up for declining domestic consumption. In addition, continued automation increases pro-

---

51. In 1966, an Equal Employment Opportunity Commission survey saw Negro participation rates in New York City for officials and managers at 0.7 percent for 100 corporations, 0.5 percent for cigarettes; for professionals, the 100 corporation average was 0.7 percent, but cigarettes stood first at 2.8 percent. For all white collar employees, the rates for the 100 corporations were 2.6 percent, for cigarettes, 2.5 percent. See *Hearings before the U.S. Equal Employment Opportunity Commission on Discrimination in White Collar Employment in New York* (Washington: Government Printing Office, 1968), pp. 648, 662, and 664. The EEOC obviously used "cigarettes" as synonomous with "tobacco" in defining the industry.

ductivity, resulting in an expanded capacity to produce with no increase in personnel, or even with a decreased labor force.

In the craft situation, not only are few Negroes qualified, but those that are continue to find intense white worker opposition to their advancement, often solidified and strengthened by craft unions. The potential for a faster rate of improvement in upgrading Negroes is not too great even with the support of the courts for special "make-up" seniority provisions, which will be discussed later in this chapter. Whether Negroes are therefore likely to continue to be concentrated in the lower rated jobs in the industry for many years to come will depend on the capacity of company affirmative action to overcome these difficult problems.

Female Employment

As noted in previous chapters, the tobacco industry has always employed a sizeable proportion both of white and Negro women. Approximately one third of the employees are women, and the industry for many years was the only which employed Negro women in large numbers.

Mechanization of the stemmeries substantially reduced Negro female job opportunities prior to 1960. The decline in the proportion of Negroes after 1932 was in part attributable to the greatly reduced employment of black women stemmery employees. In 1930 the census reported that 65.6 percent or 14,000 of the 21,444 tobacco female "laborers and operatives" in the three key states were Negro; by 1940, the total females in these classifications had declined to 17,953 and Negro women to 9,465, or 52.7 percent.[52]

Negro women continued to lose out in the tobacco industry during the next twenty years. Total tobacco employment for women in the three states (not just laborers and operatives) in 1940 was 19,485, of whom 9,770, or 50.2 percent were black; by 1950, these figures had declined to 16,234 total and 5,977 Negro, or 36.8 percent,[53] again demonstrating the disproportionate impact on Negro female employment of stemmery mechanization and rigid segregation.

------

52. *U. S. Census of Population, 1930*, State Volumes, Table 11; *1940*, State Volumes, Table 20.

53. *Ibid., 1940*, State Volumes, Table 18; *1950*, State Volumes, Table 83.

The decade of the 1950's saw a continued decline in Negro female employment, but an actual slight increase in total female jobs in the three states. Thus 18,190 female tobacco workers were reported by the 1960 census, but it is estimated that an absolute maximum of only 25 percent were black.[54]

The decline in Negro female representation in the tobacco industry probably leveled off in the 1960's, as did that of males. The EEOC data presented in Table 13 (p. 42) show Negro females comprising 22.2 percent of all female employees in the three key states as compared with an overall black ratio of 25.6 percent. Even at this figure, it is not likely that many other manufacturing industries have a larger black female share of jobs.[55] Insofar as occupational distribution is concerned, however, only 117 of the 4,400 Negro women, 2.7 percent, were salaried, whereas 82.1 percent were classified as laborers or service workers. By 1966, there was thus little change in the occupational role of the black female tobacco employee.

Table 23 shows the percentage of Negro women in each major occupational group for the three key states for the years 1964, 1966, and 1968, based upon the field sample. Again the reader should bear in mind that this sample did not include any independent stemmeries in which Negro women traditionally make up the bulk of the labor force. Hence the data underestimate the proportion of Negro females as indicated by the figure of 22.2 percent for Negro female employment in 1966 shown by Table 13 based upon the EEOC data in 1966 as compared with 15.7 percent in Table 23 for the same year, based upon the field sample.

Table 23 does show that Negro women made some gains between 1964 and 1968 both quantitatively and qualitatively in the three states. But only a very few were employed as salaried employees other than in office and clerical jobs, and the great bulk in the plants were still listed as laborers and especially service employees in 1968.

---

54. See Appendix A. The Negro female percentage has always been below that of males. Hence, 25 percent is probably an overestimate.

55. The poultry sector of the meat industry probably has a higher black ratio. See Walter A. Fogel, *The Negro in the Meat Industry*, The Racial Policies of American Industry, Report No. 12 (Philadelphia: Industrial Research Unit, Wharton School of Finance and Commerce, University of Pennsylvania, 1970).

TABLE 23. *Tobacco Industry*
Percent Negro Female Employment by Occupational Group
Major Tobacco Manufacturing States
1964, 1966, 1968

Occupational Group	Total 1964	Total 1966	Total 1968	Kentucky 1964	Kentucky 1966	Kentucky 1968	North Carolina 1964	North Carolina 1966	North Carolina 1968	Virginia 1964	Virginia 1966	Virginia 1968
Officials and managers	—	—	—	—	—	—	—	—	—	—	—	—[a]
Professionals	4.3	4.3	2.4	25.0[b]	16.7[c]	—	6.2	7.1	4.4	—	—	—
Technicians	2.1	1.3	2.1	2.7	1.2	1.9	3.3	1.7	4.1	—	1.1	—
Sales workers	—	2.7	—	—[a]	—[a]	—[a]	—	2.7	—[a]	—[a]	—[a]	—[a]
Office and clerical	2.5	2.8	4.0	3.8	3.5	4.7	1.9	2.1	3.2	2.8	3.7	5.3
Total white collar	2.4	2.6	3.6	3.8	3.2	4.1	1.9	2.1	3.2	2.1	2.6	4.1
Craftsmen	—	—	—	—	—[a]	7.6	—	—	—	—[a]	—	—[a]
Operatives	7.4	7.5	9.8	3.5	4.8	7.6	10.1	7.8	10.3	7.2	9.5	11.5
Laborers	26.4	29.1	30.1	18.6	30.3	27.8	24.6	26.3	26.6	37.1	34.2	38.8
Service workers	74.3	73.5	66.9	26.2	36.9	51.0	98.2	94.5	77.4	94.4	97.1	57.1
Total blue collar	16.4	17.9	18.4	8.5	15.5	15.7	19.5	19.1	18.4	17.4	18.5	21.4
Total	14.4	15.7	16.0	7.7	13.6	13.9	16.6	16.5	15.5	15.9	16.6	19.3

Source: Tables 17-19 and Appendix Tables B-1 - B-9.

[a] None reported of either race.
[b] One Negro of four.
[c] One Negro of six.

The consolidated reports of the tobacco companies (Table 21) show a larger number, although still very few, in salaried positions other than office and clerical, but about the same blue collar service employment and laborer concentration. The four New York City based concerns, as already noted (Table 22), have a higher office and clerical representation of Negroes than is found in the three key manufacturing states, but only 77 employees, including two Negroes in other classifications.

COMPANY DIFFERENCES

Although the tobacco companies have followed much the same path toward trying to eliminate the traditional racial-occupational segregation pattern, there have been significant variations in policies and practices. These have resulted from a variety of factors including different governmental legal tactics and pressures, union policies, civil rights actions, managerial policies, etc. Since much of what has occurred and is continuing is a matter of record, individual company names can be utilized.

R. J. Reynolds

That Reynolds is a leader in the integration of the tobacco factory work forces appears indisputable. Nevertheless, the proportion of Negroes employed at Reynolds has declined sharply over the years, and difficulty has been experienced even in the 1960's. The accomplishments and the problems at Reynolds are in some ways unique and in others typical of the industry.

Reynolds had three significant factors in its favor which aided the integration process. First, it had made several breakthroughs in the integration process in the past. As in other tobacco companies, Negroes have been employed in unskilled jobs and in the processing department all along. But over the years, Negroes have also been given the opportunity for semiskilled jobs in the white departments. The plug (chewing) and leaf departments, as well as a section of the cigarette department, became predominantly Negro. The smoking tobacco department and the remainder of the cigarette department were integrated, but the job classifications were predominantly segregated; the Negroes held the lower-classified jobs and the higher-classified jobs were reserved for the whites. Skilled Negroes had been used in segregated production rooms since 1919, and a few Negroes have been employed on cigarette machines since World War II. Thus integration in the 1960's was not totally new.

A second factor aiding the company has been its active role in the community and the strong feeling of community responsibility with which its management is imbued. Reynolds is not only the largest employer in Winston-Salem, North Carolina, but also maintains its corporate headquarters there. Company officials take an active role in community affairs, and have been strong leaders in community desegregation activities. Prior to legislation requiring the elimination of segregated state and municipal facilities, Winston-Salem integrated all public facilities except a park which had been willed to white residents and which required a court suit to open to blacks.[56]

While community desegregation was in progress; company officials met with Negro leaders in the community and laid out a program to desegregate its factories. The company's participation in community desegregation gave it additional credibility here. Moreover, the Negro leaders were aware of what in this case was Reynolds' third advantage in the movement toward desegregation—it had no union, and therefore, the status quo of the 1930's was not institutionalized, nor was there a vehicle for organized white worker opposition to desegregation which could easily be backed up by strike action or threats thereof.[57]

Perhaps, however, the fundamental reason why Reynolds was willing to move forward was that its management, realizing that it was both sound business and the right thing to do, had the foresight to seize the opportunity when it was presented. In March 1961, President Kennedy signed Executive Order 10925 strengthening the requirements for nondiscrimination by government contractors. A short time thereafter, Reynolds was scheduled to move its main production facility from downtown Winston-Salem and to start production in a new, modern, $32,000,000 plant in Whitaker Park, located just outside of that city. This plant was to be the largest cigarette manufacturing facility in the world, covering an area larger than twelve football fields, and it was planned as a showplace for the public. Each cigarette-making machine would be capable of producing more than 2,000

---

56. See "Company F. A Southern Tobacco Company" [obviously Reynolds] in Stephen Habbe, *Company Experience with Negro Employment*, Studies in Personnel Policy No. 201 (New York: National Industrial Conference Board, 1966), pp. 124-127; and Clarence N. Patrick, "Desegregation in a Southern City," *Phylon*, Vol. XXV (Fall 1964), pp. 263-269.

57. The role of the TWIU in desegregation is discussed below. That unions are not always antagonistic to civil rights progress is of course obvious, and has been pointed out in many reports in this Series.

cigarettes per minute and more than 200 packs per minute would be produced by each packaging machine. Reynolds decided that the easiest way to comply with Executive Order 10925 would be to integrate the production lines upon opening Whitaker Park.

This, then, is what was done. Each worker from the old plant who was to be transferred and each new hiree was informed of the new system in detail. So when production began in April, Negroes and whites were holding the same jobs at the same rates of pay in the same production lines. There was some apprehension among the workers, but few protested against the new system. In part, this can be attributed to the positive attitude of the community and the company toward integration. Also, there were no unions with segregated locals or departmental seniority rights. In addition, most employees desired strongly to work in the new and pleasant surroundings of the Whitaker Park facility; they preferred to stay in an integrated plant rather than quit just to escape integration.

As the Whitaker Park plant was being opened, a schedule was established to desegregate the facilities at the older plants. Drinking fountain signs were removed, walls separating the eating areas taken down, a single cafeteria line was established, and finally toilets and locker rooms were desegregated. Job integration meanwhile proceeded in the older, in town, facilities.

The company planned and monitored these personnel policies and programs through a strong centralized personnel department which does all personnel screening and placement and, in addition, makes frequent visits and checks to ascertain whether operating departments are adhering to these policies. Civil rights and industrial race relations have thus been given careful scrutiny. The personnel department also carefully reviews all discharges so that if discrimination is involved, it can be detected prior to final action.

In the early years of the desegregation policy, there was no specific policy to recruit or to promote Negroes into better jobs. Rather, they were promoted on the basis of qualifications in competition with other qualified personnel. In the early 1960's, this resulted in limited progress. Negro women were promoted to foremen on the machines and checked the output of Negro and white operators. Seven Negro technicians on the payroll and eleven Negro craftsmen were upgraded; and Negro receptionists and secretaries were employed in the corporate offices.

Most of the janitor force remained Negro as did the shipping department, which was almost 100 percent Negro with the exception of white foremen. Although the company strove to remove all-white and all-Negro teams on the machines, it did not succeed in several instances in the making and packing departments. Also, Negroes still tended to be segregated by aisle in the machine departments or within an area of machines in the department. In other departments, such as filter-making and glue, only a token representation of Negroes was found as late as 1965.

Mechanization and improved methods continued to eat into jobs at Reynolds in the early 1960's, with traditional Negro jobs disproportionately affected. As a result, the long term decline in Negro representation in the company's (and the state's) tobacco labor force had not ceased by 1965. Two years later, the declining percentages of blacks was turned around for the first time in three decades, but the Negro concentration in the lowest rated jobs continued. Reynolds decided to attempt to resolve these inequities by an entirely new, affirmative approach.

First, all employees were encouraged to fill out a thirty-six page questionnaire revealing skills, educational background, talents, interests, and aptitudes (but not race). This was worked into a computerized skills inventory which is carefully kept up to date. Then the company identified 225 job classifications and 52 lines of progression. It formalized a procedure that requires promotion of the most senior qualified person. If no qualified person is available, the Reynolds procedure requires a supervisor to select for training the most senior man who is trainable.

The program is carefully audited at the personnel department level. A supervisor who does not promote or offer training to the most senior man must file a detailed report explaining his action and obtain approval for it. In addition, supervisors must counsel employees on a regular basis and file personnel performance and development reports with the personnel department with a notation showing that the report has been discussed with the employee. Employees are also urged and counselled to enter training programs, and supervisors are regularly cautioned to increase minority representation in jobs formerly all white.

To monitor this program, Reynolds employed a native North Carolinian, Marshall B. Bass, who had entered the U.S. Army as a recruit, gone through college and Officer Candidate School, and worked up to become a colonel. Mr. Bass, a Negro, was appointed Manager, Personnel Development. He has full authority to approve or disapprove all promotions, training assignments, and policies relating to all non-officer employees, and is especially directed to see to it that no discrimination occurs.

Since this program was effectuated minority representation in all white collar jobs has risen steadily, and in the lowest rung blue collar occupations it has declined. The downturn in total Negro ratio has also been halted. Although the proportion of Negroes employed by Reynolds is now only about one-half of that which existed before stemmeries were mechanized, it remains about 25 percent—the highest of any company in the industry.

R. J. Reynolds has thus vigorously moved toward equality of opportunity. Yet many problems remain. The more skilled Negroes are difficult to recruit. More often than not, whites seeking jobs have better schooling and/or experience. Mechanization and the uncertain demand for tobacco products limit opportunities for upgrading. It will take many years to offset the long history of the racial-occupational segregation pattern.

American Brands, Inc.

American Brands, until 1969 known as American Tobacco Company, has its headquarters in New York. It operates major tobacco facilities in Richmond, Virginia, Durham and Reidsville, North Carolina, and is phasing out its operations in Louisville, Kentucky. Like all tobacco concerns, American traditionally employed whites and Negroes in accordance with the racial-occupational segregation pattern and, like all but Reynolds, it was unionized in the 1930's by the Tobacco Workers' International Union on a segregated local union basis. Moreover, American's corporate organization followed the same pattern, since a separate division, American Suppliers, processed the tobacco and then "sold" it to American tobacco for manufacturing. Since the stemmeries were operated by American Suppliers, most Negroes worked for one corporate division and whites for another within the total corporation. As already noted, in Louisville this division was compounded because the Teamsters represented the stemmery workers, and the TWIU, the manufacturing unit.

In the previous chapter, it was noted that under pressure from the President's Committee on Government Contracts (Nixon Committee), American had upgraded a few Negroes at its Richmond and Durham facilities during the 1950's. Since, however, neither of these facilities had done any hiring during most of this decade, no more progress was made, and, as a result of modernization programs, some of those upgraded (as well as many whites) were downgraded during this period.

A master contract governs relations between American and the six TWIU locals (three of each race) in Durham, Reidsville, and Richmond, with a separate agreement covering the Louisville plant. (In addition, a number of craft unions hold separate agreements at the various plants.) In 1962, the master contract governing North Carolina and Virginia plants provided for promotions and demotions on the basis of seniority, but made no mention of seniority districts or scope—that is, whether plant, job, departmental, or some other method of determining seniority prevailed.[58] In actual fact, by either agreement of the locals or custom, job seniority had always prevailed. Separate locals on the basis of race insured that promotion, transfer, and demotion were confined to the groups of classifications under the jurisdiction of each separate local. There was no provision in the labor-management agreement for transfer from one local jurisdiction to another, and by tradition there was, in fact, little or no interjurisdictional mobility except in the few instances in which management transferred employees from the operation at American Suppliers to the cigarette factory operation. Seniority areas were classified by male and female, white and Negro, and by the fabrication departments and the pre-fabrication departments.

The modernization program inaugurated by the company in the 1950's was preceded by an agreement with the TWIU not to lay off anyone because of automation. This saddled the company with considerable excess labor which had prior rights to the better jobs before Negroes or others in lower rated positions could assert upgrading rights.

A number of complaints were made to the newly created President's Committee on Equal Employment Opportunity (PCEEO) by Negro employees of American in early 1962. Government investigators placed heavy pressure on the company and TWIU to merge the local unions [59] and to eliminate separate seniority and separate facilities. The locals were merged by January 1964,

---

58. "Agreement between the American Tobacco Company and Local Nos. 182, 183, 191, 192, 204, and 216 of the Tobacco Workers' International Union, AFL-CIO, effective January 1, 1962," mimeo., Article 8.

59. The merger of local unions and the issues relating thereto are discussed in a subsequent section of this chapter.

and the separate facilities eliminated some time earlier. Seniority, however, continued to be a problem.

In the American tobacco plants, opportunities for promotions continued to be relatively infrequent. Seniority was widened and many seniority lists combined in all plants, and Negroes were promoted to once all-white jobs. Indeed, this occurred with enough frequency in Richmond that white employees charged Negroes were favored at their expense. On the other hand, Negroes, particularly in Reidsville and Durham, have charged that the existence of American Suppliers as a quasi-separate entity has acted as a barrier to their progress by providing the basis for separate seniority systems, and particularly has denied seasonal employees the opportunity to transfer to better jobs. Company and union officials deny this, pointing out that seasonal employees in American plants actually have preferential rights for open jobs in all associated tobacco manufacturing plants.

The facts appear to be that American has opened up all jobs to blacks, but that declining sales and continued automation preclude any significant opportunity for advancement. The transfer of Louisville jobs to the three other plants could create some movement. As the situation now stands, seasonal employees (mostly Negroes) are governed by a separate agreement from that covering year around employees, but seasonal workers do have prior rights to open jobs. If they accept such jobs, they give up their seasonal seniority and begin as new employees.

A court case is now pending involving the Reidsville operations, in which Negro seasonal employees are asking for transfer with full seniority rights from the seasonal operation to the full-time facility. They are basing this claim on the decision in the Philip Morris litigation [60] discussed below, which clearly did not, however, grant this privilege.

American Suppliers has been abolished as a separate entity, but the manufacturing plants and stemmeries continue under separate managements. These report to different middle managers whose supervision is unified only in the person of the Vice-President—Manufacture and Leaf in New York. Seasonal employees not only have preference for manufacturing jobs but also for any disadvantaged or hard-core training programs.

---

60. *Quarles* v. *Philip Morris, Inc.*, 279 F. Supp. 505 (E. D. Va., 1968). The pending American case in the U.S. District Court, Middle District, Greensboro Division, is *Russell et al.* v. *The American Tobacco Company*, Civil Action No. C-2-G-68.

Within manufacturing plants, American and the TWIU have agreed to plantwide seniority which does tend to favor long service but once discriminated against black employees. Thus, except where there is an agreed upon and extensive progression and learning period necessary to qualification, as in the case of machine adjusters or craftsmen, anyone with the requisite plant-wide seniority can successfully bid on a job. The company is required to train that person even though previously qualified and trained persons, including those once downgraded from the open job, are available but have less plantwide seniority. The only qualification required is the capacity to perform reasonably the duties of the job after training.

At the present time, lines of seniority at American plants are merged and Negroes are working in jobs formerly reserved for whites. The company, like others in the industry, has attempted, with some success, to employ Negroes in higher rated jobs, particularly in white collar and sales jobs. Employment is not expanding, however, and, as in the rest of the industry, integration occurred after many Negroes had been eliminated from the company's work force by a combination of automation, segregation, and job denial over a long period. Today, American's Negro work force is about 20 percent of the total, putting it slightly below Reynolds and Liggett & Myers in this regard.

Liggett & Myers

Liggett & Myers' principal tobacco manufacturing operations are in Richmond and Durham. Its past history is quite like that of American, with employment historically segregated in accordance with the industry's pattern, and, since the 1930's, union relations characterized by segregated locals and seniority. Similarly, Liggett & Myers broke the segregation pattern and upgraded a few Negroes to formerly all-white jobs under pressure from the Nixon Committee in the 1950's, but its declining employment has precluded the potential for great change.

The local unions at the Liggett & Myers Richmond and Durham plants, as at American facilities, bargained jointly. One Negro and one white local existed at Richmond, but at Durham there were two Negro locals and one white. One Negro local (No. 194) represented seasonal employees and others in the processing department, the other (No. 208), represented those in the manufacturing department and other full-time employees. In 1937, Local 194 had approximately 2,800 members; No. 208

had 800 members; and No. 176, the white local, 1,600 members. In this situation (and probably others), union segregation was, among other things, initially a device to preserve white hegemony.

In the late 1940's and early 1950's, Negroes were laid off in large numbers, particularly at the Durham works, but also in Richmond, while jobs under the jurisdiction of the white local increased. Thus a statement of Local 208 claimed that in 1950:

. . . approximately 1,800 Negroes, members of local 194, were laid off. Cut-offs and layoffs did not affect many of the white employees, members of local 176. . . . Instead there was an actual increase in the number of white employees. Negroes with more than 20 years of seniority were cut-off while whites were being hired into the tobacco industry for the first time in jobs at a higher classification and at a higher rate of pay, but equivalent in skill to those from which Negroes had been cut-off.[61]

What actually occurred was that Liggett & Myers began moving its major stemmery operations out of Durham in 1950, operating only on a short seasonal basis between 1950 and 1964. Stemmery operations were closed permanently in 1964. In addition, it abolished the night shift in the blending operation in 1962. All these actions, although dictated by business conditions, substantially reduced Negro employment.

These reductions led to the pressures which first brought the Nixon Committee and later the PCEEO into the picture. At the insistence of the latter agency, Liggett & Myers opened up all jobs to Negroes and whites, and with the national officials of the TWIU, pressured the local unions to merge.

The Richmond locals of the TWIU at Liggett & Myers did merge, but at Durham one Negro local held out. In 1962 new seniority agreements had been negotiated at Durham which in effect gave existing employees rights to jobs in departments other than those for which their local union bargained on the basis of seniority *after* incumbents, as follows:

1. Local 176—The names of all regular employees on the seniority lists of Locals 208 and 194 were combined in order of

---

61. From a statement by Local No. 208 to a special fact finder appointed by PCEEO. Much of our material comes from this proceeding, which was continued by the Office of Federal Contract Compliance, successor to PCEEO. Additional facts were obtained from interviews with Liggett & Myers and TWIU officials, Durham and Washington, D.C., November 14 and December 3, 1969, and from court proceedings cited in note 62, below.

employment dates and added to the bottom of the seniority list for Local 176 jobs.

2. Local 208—Locals 176 and 194 seniority lists were combined in order of employment dates and added to the seniority list of Local 208 jobs.

3. Local 194—Locals 176 and 208 seniority lists were combined in order of employment dates and added to the seniority list of Local 194 jobs.

Prior to this action, strict local union seniority had prevailed at Liggett & Myers, except that members of Local 194, the Durham Negro local in processing, had preference for open jobs under the jurisdiction of Local 208, the other Durham Negro local, which members of the latter did not desire, or could not fill. This allowed seasonal employees to obtain full year jobs.

The national TWIU and Liggett & Myers officials had hoped that the 1962 agreement would lead to a merger of the locals. Local 208 officials, however, declined to accept merger on this basis. There then began a long legal battle involving the company, the union, and several civil rights and government agencies.

The company was on the spot because the PCEEO and its successor, the Office of Federal Contract Compliance (OFCC), took the position that Liggett & Myers was in noncompliance with Executive Order No. 10925, and therefore, potentially ineligible for government contracts if it dealt with segregated local unions. The officers of TWIU felt that segregated locals were an embarrassment, as we shall discuss later in this chapter. Nevertheless, aided by attorney Floyd McKissick, later president of the Congress on Racial Equality (CORE), Local 208 resisted pressure for merger until it could secure what it regarded as a more satisfactory arrangement on seniority and on representation in local union offices. Meanwhile Local 194 was merged into Local 176 at a sparsely attended meeting. Litigation over this was threatened but apparently did not materialize. Alleged participation of Local 176 officials in White Citizens' Council activities in Durham certainly did not decrease the apprehensions of blacks concerning local union mergers.

In 1964, the international TWIU officials ordered Local 208 to merge with Local 176, and served notice that a trusteeship would be imposed if it did not do so. Local 208 officials obtained an ex parte injunction restraining the international officials from lifting Local 208's charter. On the subsequent hearing, the injunction was modified and extended until Local 208 could exhaust its internal remedies. This it did, first with a hearing presided over by George Benjamin, who was then the senior Negro officer of the TWIU. Mr. Benjamin, then the TWIU president, and finally the 1964 TWIU convention, all upheld the action which proposed to put Local 208 into trusteeship, then lift its charter and merge it with Local 176.[62]

In the meantime, Liggett & Myers was faced with bargaining demands by Local 176, which now claimed to represent all bargaining unit employees in Durham. Given the predominance of white employees and a split among Negroes over the merger question, Local 176 easily proved majority status by signed authorization cards. Anxious to see the end of the racial local situation and believing that a National Labor Relations Board election campaign would only exacerbate existing racial tensions, the company recognized Local 176 as exclusive bargaining agent for all Durham represented employees. A joint contract for Richmond and Durham was negotiated with Locals 176 and 177 (Richmond). One Negro from Richmond was on the bargaining committee, but none from Durham. Local 208 officials then filed a charge with the National Labor Relations Board charging the company and the union with unfair labor practices. The District Court then continued the injunction against lifting 208's charter until the NLRB had exhausted jurisdiction over the local's charges.

At this point, the President's Committee on Equal Employment Opportunity, whose simplistic view that the abolition of separate racial locals must, of itself, improve Negro job opportunities resulted in the controversy reaching its high pitch, appointed veteran labor relations arbitrator and mediator, Ronald W. Haughton, to try to resolve the dispute. The NLRB took no action on Local 208's charges while the Haughton proceeding was pending.

62. Transcipt and order in *Daye* v. *Tobacco Workers International Union,* Civil Action No. 1924-64, U.S. Dist. Ct., D.C., August 6, 14, 17, 1964, February 11, 1966, and April 1, 1968. See also "Negro Seniority Fight Raises Broad Rights Issue," *New York Times,* December 13, 1964. According to this story, a member of the TWIU at the convention told the reporter that "if we ever merge locals 176 and 208, it will be the first organization in the world composed of Negroes, members of the White Citizens Council and the Ku Klux Klan." The *Times* reporter obviously was unaware of similar situations in the paper, rubber, automobile, steel, textile, building trades, and many other local unions in the South.

After initial investigations, Mr. Haughton, whose appointment was continued by the Office of Federal Contract Compliance, successor to the PCEEO, held hearings over a nine-month period in 1965, and issued his report on April 8, 1966. In it, he found that the seniority article noted above, which tied together the former seniority arrangements of the prior segregated era were not discriminatory on their face, but that they tended to perpetuate past seniority practices and to maintain a kind of super-seniority for whites in the better jobs. Instead, he recommended that jobs be assigned in the future on the basis of seniority regardless of former local union jurisdiction (that is, plantwide seniority), except in machine line progressions where orderly on-the-job training required that job seniority prevail in promotion from the bottom job to the next higher, etc. Under this recommendation, plant seniority would, of course, govern openings on the bottom machine progression job. In order to facilitate integration, Mr. Haughton proposed a system of maintaining or "red-circling" wages so that Negroes who entered the bottom of a machine progression as a means of qualifying for top jobs would not have to accept a reduction in pay.

Following receipt of the Haughton report, a long series of bargaining conferences took place. An agreement was finally reached which actually went beyond the Haughton recommendations. It provided for plantwide seniority except for two ladders of progression—one on packing machines, the other on cigarette making machines. The senior employee, regardless of race or sex, can bid on any job outside the two progression ladders. Moreover, once an employee successfully bids into the bottom job of either progression ladder and works in this capacity for 160 days or more, he moves up the progression ladder by plant seniority.

White employees were induced to accept this agreement because the TWIU and Liggett & Myers agreed to "red circle" any employee bumped out of position as a result of the agreement up to a maximum of 23 cents per hour. Local 208 officials had an additional inducement to agree because they had been losing their members to Local 176 and the local was close to the TWIU constitutional minimum of ten members by the time that it agreed to merge. If its membership had fallen below the ten member minimum, its charter would have been subject to automatic forfeiture.

The last segregated local in the TWIU—Local 208—thus merged with Local 176. On May 31, 1967, the merger and the above summarized agreement were noted in a telegram from the Director of the Office of Federal Contract Compliance which stated that as a result thereof, Liggett & Myers was in compliance with Executive Order 11246. The National Labor Relations Board's General Counsel dismissed Local 208's charge and the United States District Court dissolved the restraining order.

Unfortunately, the civil rights litigation at Liggett & Myers did not end. The Equal Employment Opportunity Commission, after receiving a complaint, demanded that Liggett & Myers supply it with information dating back to the period when the PCEEO (later OFCC) was investigating the matter. The company demurred, pointing out that it was found in compliance with the executive order on May 31, 1967, and proposing that the EEOC confine its investigation to the period since that date. The EEOC refused and won a court order that the company produce its files.[63] That order is presently being appealed. Given the EEOC's backlog of complaints and the long litigation that ensued involving another governmental civil rights agency, together with its successor, its special fact finder, the National Labor Relations Board, and a United States District Court, one can well wonder what purpose is being fulfilled by a rehash of the matter.

Another reason why the EEOC's insistence on an investigation of matters prior to June 1967 is not easily comprehended, is that few jobs are in fact at stake. Liggett & Myers in Durham has not employed anyone since 1956 and few, if any, in Richmond since then. The situation is not likely to change since the company has been losing market position for a number of years and is increasing the speed of its cigarette machines and introducing other improvements. Like other companies, it has attempted to employ Negro sales personnel and other white collar employees, with limited success. Liggett & Myers now has a Negro complement of about 20 percent, which is approximately equal to American and slightly below Reynolds. Given the lack of job openings, the Negro employees of Liggett & Myers are likely to continue to be concentrated in the lower rated jobs for the forseeable future.

---

63. *Equal Employment Opportunity Commission* v. *Liggett & Myers Tobacco Company*, U.S. Dist. Ct., Mid. Dist., N.C., No. C-126-D-69, September 30, 1969

Brown & Williamson

Brown & Williamson operates major plants in Petersburg, Virginia and Louisville, Kentucky, with a smaller facility in Winston-Salem. Petersburg is a city moving toward a majority Negro population, and Brown & Williamson there has a sizeable Negro labor force—about one-third of the total. At Louisville, however, less than 10 percent of the work force is black. Separate locals existed at Petersburg (but not at Louisville) with the usual racial job division, separate seniority, etc.

When locals of Brown & Williamson in Petersburg were merged, the Negro local survived—one of only two situations where this occurred. (The other was at United States Tobacco, Richmond.) Moreover, the president of the former black local, Oliver Shaw, became president of the new body and in 1968 was also elected an international vice-president.

Of special interest is the fact that the Petersburg locals were able to merge on a basis that set the stage for the Haughton proposal and the subsequent Liggett & Myers settlement. In 1964, these locals merged and agreed with the company on a seniority arrangement which opens up all but machine progression jobs on the basis of plantwide seniority. After an employee has been on a job for three months, he can utilize plant seniority for promotion to open jobs. On layoffs, plant seniority governs in all cases.

This agreement was worked out with no outside assistance in a plant that has as large a black ratio as any in the industry except stemmeries. Undoubtedly, the fact that the company has been gaining a large share of the market, and hiring instead of laying off, has helped. Negro representation in the total company is, however, only about one-half that of the Petersburg plant and considerably less than that of the companies previously discussed.

P. Lorillard—Departmental Segregation and Seniority

The major facilities of P. Lorillard are in Greensboro, North Carolina, where the company transferred its former Jersey City, New Jersey operations in 1956, and in Louisville. The former plant now has a Negro complement of about 20 percent, the latter, less than one-fourth that. Yet it was problems at the former which generated the most heat and led to the most improvement.

At Jersey City, Lorillard followed the occupational pattern of the industry despite the location of its plant until directed to cease violating New Jersey civil rights laws in 1951. Thus the files of the then New Jersey Division Against Discrimination contain this note from the Division's assistant director:

We did discover . . . the existence of a form of racial segregation which the union and the employees have permitted to exist from the very beginning of this plant's operations.[64]

By 1954, this same official wrote the company noting considerable progress in integration, but still a heavy concentration of Negroes in the leaf and cutting departments and an equally heavy ratio of whites in making and packing.[65] Soon thereafter, of course, the company began its move South, where it again firmly adhered to southern customs, as it had continued to do in Louisville. It set up the new plant on a strictly segregated basis and set the stage for rigid departmental seniority contract provisions —a provision that is inherently discriminatory when combined with a discriminatory hiring pattern, but which would not necessarily be so when employment is conducted without discrimination. At its Greensboro plant, Lorillard employed Negroes only for jobs in leaf processing, blending, cutting, stripping, receiving, and service departments.[66] The last named included janitors and sweepers and therefore departmental lines prevented Negroes employed in these occupational roles from advancing to better jobs.

The Greensboro Lorillard plant was organized by the TWIU soon after its establishment. On instructions from the TWIU general president, it was organized on an integrated basis and two Negroes were represented on the first seven-man negotiating committee.[67] But the white majority on the TWIU negotiating committee proposed, and the company accepted, seniority provisions which limited movement to occupational groups within

---

64. From the files of the New Jersey Division, in the author's possession.

65. *Ibid.* The situation in Jersey City was confirmed by the testimony of Carl Fieg, formerly factory manager at the Jersey City plant of P. Lorillard, and later director of manufacturing for the company in *Robinson et al.* v. *P. Lorillard et al.*, U.S. Dist. Ct., Mid. Dist., N.C., Case No. C-14-G-66, May 5-7, 1969; transcript of testimony, pp. 248-260, 265-268.

66. See especially the testimony of the then personnel manager of the Lorillard plant, *Robinson* v. *P. Lorillard, op. cit.*, pp. 239-247. Helping to maintain segregation was the North Carolina Employment Service, then also racially segregated and highly discriminatory.

67. *Ibid.*, testimony of Lionel J. Dugas, TWIU organizer, p. 355

departments. White members of the negotiating committee and former local union officials later testified that this proposal emanated from the desire to prevent Negroes from advancing to better jobs.[68] This allegation was denied by the first local union president, but in fact, the white members of the negotiating committee did meet for lunch at a cafeteria which Negroes were not allowed to use, and there strategy was apparently determined to accomplish their purpose.[69]

In addition to the issue of Negro rights, the departmental seniority issue at Lorillard's Greensboro plant involved a fundamental divergence of views among the white employees. Lorillard's "Old Gold" brand was the company's biggest seller when it opened the Greensboro plant. Then on 9 July 1958, the *Reader's Digest* carried an article which seemed to indicate that Lorillard's new "Kent" filter cigarette had the most effective restraint against harmful tars and nicotine. "Kent" sales and production expanded rapidly. Since then, "Old Gold" sales have continued to decline, and "Kent" has been the company's best seller.[70] The result has been that employees in the "Old Gold" making department, including some who came South with the company and who once saw departmental seniority to their advantage, soon joined forces with the Negro employees in demanding plant-wide seniority. The filter department employees, however, were a clear majority, and so the departmental seniority was maintained until governmental intervention following numerous complaints.

The first complaints were made to the Nixon Committee in 1958 by Negroes. This resulted in two Negroes being upgraded to then all-white departments prior to 1960. Further complaints to the PCEEO in 1961 resulted in eleven more upgradings, this time of Negro women. Then in the 1961-62 negotiations, the company and the TWIU abolished job seniority, but retained the strict departmental seniority. By this time, the company had ceased to confine Negroes and whites to segregated departments.

---

68. *Ibid.*, testimony of Lois N. Burnside, pp. 104-126; Sterling Caviness, pp. 126-133; and James R. Lee, Jr., pp. 133-147. Also affidavits filed with the National Labor Relations Board in the author's possession.

69. *Ibid.*, and testimony of Albert W. Thompson, *Robinson v. P. Lorillard*, *op. cit.*, pp. 301-316.

70. In 1969, "Kent" ranked seventh among all cigarette brands in sales, "Old Gold," nineteenth, and "Newport," another Lorillard filter, twenty-first. In 1968, "Newport" sales led "Old Gold." *Business Week* (December 1969), p. 83.

If, however, a person elected to transfer from one department to another, he would still be required under this agreement to give up all seniority in his old department and begin as a new employee in the department to which he transferred.

Under strong pressure from PCEEO, the company unilaterally granted employees the right to return to former departments with seniority intact if they elected to transfer to another department and then were laid off because of lack of work. The TWIU protested this action, took it to arbitration and won the case. In the 1965 negotiations, however, the TWIU agreed to this transfer provision. Employees who transferred started as the lowest ranking employees in the new department. Employees who were on layoff status were then given preference for any job openings in other departments, but their right to return with accumulated seniority, if recalled to their original department was limited to a two-year period.

While the difficulties over seniority continued, Lorillard, under PCEEO pressure, integrated its cafeteria in 1961, and then after North Carolina abolished its segregation laws in 1963, toilets and locker rooms. White workers boycotted the cafeteria for a time, but no incidents occurred, and the boycott soon lost effectiveness.

Throughout the period from 1963 to 1966, Negroes continued to lodge complaints with PCEEO, its successor, the Office of Federal Contract Compliance (OFCC), and with the Equal Employment Opportunity Commission, and also with the National Labor Relations Board. The EEOC found "probable cause" that discrimination existed, and the already-noted court case was filed, which led to the seniority system being declared discriminatory and the substitution of plantwide seniority therefor.[71]

White employees of the "Old Gold" departments also complained to the NLRB, charging, as did the Negroes, that the seniority arrangements represented lack of fair representation by their bargaining agent, the TWIU and its Local No. 317. Actually, movements of Negroes out of traditional jobs were occurring by 1966, as black employees took advantage of the new provision which permitted them to transfer without loss of seniority rights in their original departments. Transfers, however, were limited not only by what may have been a lack of enthusiasm on the part of the company to upset its collective bargaining relationships, but also by a lack of job openings. As a matter of fact,

---

71. *Robinson* v. *P. Lorillard, op. cit.*, transcript, pp. 323-354. The final court decision was issued on March 11, 1970.

one government investigator interviewed emphasized that even with plantwide seniority, there would be little movement of Negroes, since layoffs and low turnover kept new plant jobs at a minimum.[72]

Nevertheless, by 1968, Lorillard had made considerable progress in integration of Greensboro. It doubled its percentage of Negroes over the former ratio of 10 percent. Employing Dr. Julius Thomas, former industrial secretary of the National Urban League as a consultant, Lorillard added a number of white collar employees to its staff at Greensboro and in the New York office, and began an apprentice program in order to train potential Negro craftsmen. The bulk of its Negro employees, however, continued to remain in the lowest classifications.

Lorillard opened a new plant in the mid-1950's on the assumption that a racial-occupational segregation pattern, already under strong attack, would nevertheless endure. Its lack of foresight provided for a smooth initial relationship with its white-dominated local union, but resulted in much difficulty later on, not only with the Negro minority, but also with senior white employees. They, like the Negroes, were locked into less advantaged employment situations by a rigid departmental seniority system that could not be defended on the basis of job requirements or in-plant training needs.

As so often seems to happen, Lorillard's major problems did not occur at the plant in which the poorer integration situation existed. The ratio of Negroes at its Louisville plant in 1968 remained about 5 percent, one-fourth that at its Greensboro operation. Nor had the Louisville plant made any meaningful progress in upgrading blue collar workers nor employing Negro salaried personnel. Yet agitation for change, or involvement of government agencies therein, was as conspicuous by its absence at Louisville as by its presence in Greensboro.

Philip Morris—the "Rightful Place" Doctrine

Philip Morris operates several major facilities in Richmond and Louisville. As of 1968, Philip Morris' Negro employment was the lowest of the major producers, the only one below 15 percent. In both Louisville and Richmond plants, however, Negro employment was considerably above that figure. In its

---

72. Interview, March 1967. Since then Lorillard sales, and presumably jobs, have further declined.

Richmond plants, aided by a tight labor market and the fastest expanding sales of any cigarette company, there was a Negro ratio well over 15 percent. It was in Richmond that a key court case was generated, of great significance not only for the tobacco industry, but for industry generally.[73]

Essentially, Philip Morris followed the same employment practices as did other tobacco manufacturers. In 1955, as a result of President Eisenhower's Executive Order No. 10599, which established the Nixon Committee, the first thirteen Negroes were assigned to the Richmond plant's fabrication department. As a result of Executive Order No. 10925 of 1961 and the work of the PCEEO, Philip Morris began to move toward nondiscriminatory hiring by what the District Court termed "token hiring of Negroes in fabrication" from 1963 to 1967. On the other hand, the court noted that

Negroes have been appointed foremen in the stemmery, the blended leaf section, the wrapping section and the storage and dressing section of the company's 20th Street plant [Richmond]. Other Negroes have been placed as in export superintendent and in the quality control sections. The company has recruited Negroes from colleges to enter its management trainee program. Negroes are employed at the executive level in the sales program.[74]

Philip Morris' Richmond employees were originally represented by segregated locals. In 1963, they merged. Negroes have been represented on the bargaining committee of the merged local, but not as officers.

Prior to 1957, the wages of Negroes and whites employed in the same occupations but in different departments were unequal. Wages were equalized between 1957 and 1959, with two exceptions for which the District Court ordered equalization. Beyond these two wage rate situations, the court found no extant discrimination. It did find, however, that "the restrictive departmental transfer and seniority provisions of the collective bargaining agreement are intentional, unlawful employment practices because they are imposed on a departmental structure that was organized on a racially segregated basis." [75] Through this

---

73. *Quarles* v. *Philip Morris, Inc., loc. cit.* Our facts are based largely on the briefs and decision in this proceeding.

74. *Ibid.*

75. *Ibid.* The intellectual basis of the court's decision is found in note, "Title VII, Seniority Discrimination and the Incumbent Negro," *Harvard Law Review*, Vol. LXXX (April 1967), pp. 1260 ff.

decision, the stage was set for a challenge of seniority arrangements in other tobacco plants, for the successful challenge to seniority provisions in the paper industry, discussed in the paper study of this Series, and probably for similar challenges elsewhere.

Originally, Philip Morris operated under strict departmental seniority, which was first modified for whites, then eventually for Negroes. Because its Richmond facilities are in seven locations within that city, departmental seniority was a natural development, and, in the absence of discriminatory employment practices, would not have been considered invidious in any manner. But the court concluded that the Civil Rights Act "does not require that Negroes be preferred over white employees who possess employment seniority. It is also apparent that Congress did not intend to freeze an entire generation of Negro employees into discriminatory patterns that existed before the act." [76] Accordingly, the court did not disturb the departmental seniority system as such. Moreover, it excluded seasonal stemmery employees from relief on the grounds that they were temporary employees. It provided that all other Negro employees employed prior to January 1, 1966, who were not hired directly into, or who were not transferred in a nondiscriminatory manner into, formerly all white departments, "shall be given an opportunity to transfer to the fabrication or warehouse, shipping and receiving departments to fill vacancies if they elect to transfer and if they are qualified for the jobs they seek." [77]

To accomplish this purpose, the court ordered the company to screen its Negro employees "of the affected class," and to list those who desire to transfer and are eligible on the same basis as white employees are deemed eligible for such work. When a vacancy occurs, the company is required to offer it to the qualified employee, white or black, with the greatest company (Richmond area) seniority. Members of the affected class "shall have departmental seniority computed from their employment seniority date." [78] This they carry with them as a seniority credit to make up for past discrimination. If they fail to qualify for promotion or transfer after a fair trial, they can return

---

76. *Quarles* v. *Philip Morris, loc. cit.*

77. *Ibid.*

78. *Ibid.*

to the former jobs, without loss of seniority. The court also provided:

> For every person transferred under these procedures from the prefabrication department, the company may hire a replacement from the street, and to that extent its obligation under the collective bargaining agreement to hire into prefabrication from the semmery is modified. This provision is designed to prevent the company's new labor pool from being restricted to seasonal employees.[79]

No appeal was taken by the company or the TWIU from this decision. Management and the union are apparently living with it without difficulty. Although the *Quarles* decision gave greater opportunities to some of the black Philip Morris employees, it limited those of many others—a fact largely unnoticed to date. For the decision provided that seasonal employees have less rights to full-time jobs than they formerly had (or now have in American or Liggett & Myers plants, for example). Moreover, although the complainants in the *Russell* case involving American are demanding that seasonal employees be included in the "affected class" and given plantwide seniority, such employees were specifically excluded from exercising plantwide seniority by the *Quarles* decision. Finally, *Quarles* gave seasonal employees preferential rights only to every other full-time job opening, whereas previously they had such rights to any such openings. This came out clearly in the second big case involving Philip Morris.

Philip Morris—the "Rightful Place" of Seasonal Employees

Philip Morris' other major location is in Louisville, where in 1944 it acquired the former Axton-Fischer Tobacco Company. The latter concern had almost literally maintained the Tobacco Workers' International Union during the 1920's, being the only concern of size which then recognized the TWIU. Philip Morris took over from Axton-Fischer its labor contracts with TWIU Local 16 (white) and Local 72 (Negro), plus contracts with seven craft unions.[80]

Until 1952, Philip Morris purchased most of its tobacco for the Louisville plant from independent stemmeries. Its employees

---

79. *Ibid.*

80. *Carr et al.* v. *Philip Morris, Inc., et al.*, Complaint No. 103-E, Kentucky Commission on Human Rights, transcript of testimony, September 8-10, 23, 26, 1969, Vol. I, pp. 5-6. Most of our facts are based on this six volume transcript and the pertinent exhibits.

were thus all full time, with Negroes used in some prefabrication work, janitorial duties, and in other traditional jobs, but with more whites than is typical in North Carolina or Virginia utilized in blending and cutting departments. Intraplant movement, as described in the Liggett & Myers situation, was based on local union seniority. Negroes had seniority rights only in Local 72 jobs; whites, in Local 16 jobs. In addition, departmental restrictions on movement also existed.

In 1952, Philip Morris opened a new "green leaf" stemmery to handle tobacco purchased directly after harvesting, and a warehouse. Both were located in Louisville, but at a considerable distance from the main plant. Jurisdiction over the seasonal employees in the stemmery and over the few permanent ones in the warehouse was given to the black local (No. 72). Contracts were negotiated which gave no rights in the main plant to seasonal employees. All employees in the main plant retained their full-time jobs; the labor force, entirely Negro, for the stemmery was all newly recruited.

In 1957, partially as a result of contracts with the Nixon Committee which, it will be recalled, handled equal employment matters during the Eisenhower Administration, Philip Morris agreed to permit some seasonal employees to transfer to the main plant. Since racial segregation was being maintained, such transfers could be made only to jobs within the jurisdiction of Local 72. Transferees obtained seniority in the main plant as of the date of their transfer there, receiving no credit for seasonal employment. They were, however, permitted to bump back into the stemmery if laid off at the main plant.[81]

At first, only men in the stemmery were selected on a seniority basis to be transferred to the main plant. In 1960, at the request of the longtime (now retired) Negro vice-president of the TWIU, George Benjamin, a few women were selected for main plant jobs by the plant manager of the stemmery, with the approval of the Local 72 president. Later all selections were on a seniority basis. The company reserved the right (as it still did in 1969) to employ persons directly into the main plant from the street. Its policy has been to consider stemmery employment needs also and not to restrict its main plant hiring to its seasonal labor force. Thus an employee who was hired

---

81. *Carr* v. *Philip Morris, op. cit.*, testimony of Walter Reeb, stemmery plant manager, Vol. IV, pp. 738-823; Catherine M. L. Northington, former president of Local 72, Vol. III, pp. 730-738; Vol. IV, pp. 471-506.

into the Philip Morris main plant with no previous company
experience on December 1, 1968, would have seniority as of that
date, whereas an employee who had done seasonal stemmery
work since 1962, but did not enter the main plant until December 2, 1968, would have seniority in the main plant from the
latter date and could be laid off while the newly-hired worker
remained on the job. On the other hand, only the former seasonal employee could bump back into the stemmery during the
eight months in which the stemmery was operating.[82]

Beginning in 1961 with the establishment of President Kennedy's President's Committee on Equal Employment Opportunity,
successor to the Nixon Committee, Philip Morris began desegre-
gating its Louisville operations and the TWIU commenced push-
ing for the merger of its locals. In October 1961, the company
and the unions agreed to permit employees in other departments
to transfer to the cigarette department in stipulated numbers.
At that time, all permanent Negro employees in the main plant
were in what was called the "sundry department." They, like
white employees, were thus permitted to transfer to the preferred department, cigarette making. Moreover, the new under-
standing provided: "In the event Sundry Job personnel decline
transfer to the Cigarette Department, Stemmery male or female,
as needed, will be permitted to transfer to the Cigarette Department." [83]

This, of course, was progress, but it discriminated against
Negroes in two ways. First, stemmery employees were given
preference for cigarette making jobs only if sundry department
personnel—that is, other Negroes—declined transfer to such jobs,
but were given no such preference when other (white) employees declined transfers. Second, the October 1961 arrangement
contained this clause:

> When employees transfer outside of the jurisdiction of their re-
> spective local unions, their departmental seniority will begin on the
> date they begin work therein. When employees transfer within the
> jurisdiction of their respective local unions, they will carry their
> seniority to the job to which they transfer.[84]

What this clause meant was that transferring white employees
carried their Local 16 seniority with them unless they trans-

82. *Ibid.*

83. *Ibid.*, Vol. I, p. 53.

84. *Ibid.*, Vol. I, p. 54.

ferred to the sundry department, which none did. On the other hand, transferring Negro employees were given no credit for their time worked in the sundry department prior to their transfer. This was obviously and invidiously discriminatory.

At this time also, Philip Morris announced that it would hire whites into the stemmery and Negroes into former white jobs in the main plant, but it was not until 1963 that any substantial integration progress was made and the first Negroes employed off the street into anything but the sundry department. In 1963 also, the same employment tests and qualifications were applied to stemmery employment as to that in the main plant. During this period, cafeterias, restrooms, etc. were desegrated as well.[85]

As the company was altering its policies, Locals 16 and 72 were negotiating for a merger. Some members of Local 72 apparently desired to hold out for stemmery employees to obtain seniority credit in the main plant for work performed in seasonal jobs and for assurance of at least one major office in the merged union; others were apparently ready to settle for equal seniority within the main plant by giving sundry department employees the same seniority rights as whites who transferred from one former white department to another. The division within the black local weakened its position. It apparently voted to merge but also to refrain from executing the merger.

While this was occurring, Local 72 failed to comply with the TWIU's constitutional requirement for election of officers. After a hearing, the international union placed Local 72 into trusteeship, appointed a merger committee, and effectuated the merger. Former and existing sundry department employees were given, retroactively, full seniority rights in transfers. Negroes have since served as stewards and bargaining committee members, and as trustee and sergeant-at-arms, but no higher offices in the surviving local, No. 16.[86]

Today, both the main plant and the stemmery are well integrated. Like its Richmond factory, the company's Louisville facility has expanded and increased its proportion of Negroes

---

85. *Ibid.*, testimony of John Cox, Personnel and Labor Relations Manager, Vol. III, pp. 506-592; Vol. IV, pp. 671-710.

86. The merger issue was discussed from all points of view in testimony in *Carr* v. *Philip Morris, op. cit.*, testimony of James Juleson, Vol. II, pp. 350-429; Catherine M. L. Northington, *loc. cit.*; B. T. Curtis, Vol. V, pp. 1041-1119 and Vol. VI, pp. 1237-1252.

to over 20 percent. There is thus no claim of existing discrimination. Rather what the complaints before the Kentucky Commission on Civil Rights are demanding is an extension of the "rightful place" doctrine, enunciated in the *Quarles* case, by applying it to a "class" of seasonal employees. Specifically, they are requesting the Kentucky Commission to give additional seniority rights to Negro seasonal employees hired by the stemmery between its opening in 1952 and October 10, 1961, when Philip Morris began its integration program in Louisville, or to those employed prior to various dates in 1963 or 1964 when alleged discrimination is claimed to have existed.

Whatever date is picked, it is admitted that there is no civil rights case in the denial of main plant seniority to stemmery employees after racial discrimination was no longer a factor. The contention of the complainants, however, is that the before and after time periods are different because those hired during the earlier period were denied opportunities in the main plant because of their race; hence they now carry a present disadvantage based on prior discrimination.

What is at stake is how far the "rightful place" doctrine is to be carried. If it is applied, how far back should it go? Should seasonal employees be compensated for discrimination in hiring and promotion in a period that some complainants say ended four years prior to the effective date of Title VII of the federal Civil Rights Act or even a longer time prior to the very similar Kentucky Act under which the litigation was brought? If so, should they be given full seniority for an average of two-thirds of a year's work? Should they be given proportional credit related to their typical year's service? These are some of the questions before the Kentucky Commission. It is likely that whatever its decision, the issue will be appealed and eventually resolved in court.

TWIU RACIAL POLICIES IN THE 1960's

In the 1960's, the TWIU succeeded in eliminating all its segregated locals, with only the Negro local of Liggett & Myers workers in Durham, North Carolina, offering any strong resistance. TWIU officials had desired to end this embarrassing practice of segregation earlier. No segregated locals were given charters after World War II (few of any type were organized after that date), and as noted, the new Lorillard local in Greensboro was integrated from the start. Moreover, many locals in the border city of Louisville were nearly all integrated from their inception. In a strong editorial in the *Tobacco Worker* in 1957, the president of the TWIU emphasized the union policy:

> America is opportunity, where a man's station in life is what he makes it and not what his birth might indicate . . . America is the conscience that pushes us and those with whom we associate in the world toward greater justice for all men, no matter what their creed or color.[88]

The TWIU national officials also felt that segregated locals divided employees and the union and weakened their bargaining power. Accordingly, when the PCEEO took the position, beginning in 1961, that a company would be ineligible for government contracts if it dealt with segregated locals, the TWIU national officials began their campaign of education, persuasion, and direct action to merge the black and white locals. Companies, anxious to avoid complications in government contracts, added their influence. In two cases already noted—the Brown & Williamson locals in Petersburg and those at United States Tobacco in Richmond—smaller white locals merged into Negro locals with Negro local presidents. In all other cases, the Negro locals disbanded and merged into the white locals. By the time that Title VII of the Civil Rights Act of 1964 became effective, only the black local at Liggett & Myers in Durham held out.

In the paper industry study, it was noted that the integration of racially segregated local unions, the simplistic views of some governmental civil rights functionaries to the contrary notwithstanding, is not necessarily always in the interest of the black unionists. To be sure, the purpose of these segregated locals was originally clearly and avowedly discriminatory—to control the work and opportunities of Negroes, and in some cases, to deny them control of racially mixed unions. Segregated unions added another fence around the industry's segregation pattern and served both to institutionalize it and to make it more difficult to change. Yet, it has been the segregated locals which have developed Negro leadership and provided the mainsprings of protest which have led to the significant changes of the last few years. The fact that some of the white union officials were anxious to merge locals lends some credence to the views ex-

---

88. *Tobacco Worker*, February 1957. (This was Vol. I, No. 7, of a new issue of the oft-started, oft-abandoned journal.)

pressed in 1964 by John H. Wheeler, president of a major Negro-owned bank in Durham, North Carolina, and then a member of PCEEO. Stating that the "new policies on racial matters at the national level" were not being honored by local unions "because their members still have strong views of an entirely different nature," Mr. Wheeler declared that in the tobacco industry

. . . the white segregated locals (whose membership lists are overwhelmingly larger than those of the Negro locals) are moving to take over the Negro locals in order to prevent them from filing complaints with the President's Committee on Equal Employment Opportunity. Wherever this operation has been successfully engineered, the Negro members are out-numbered and are no longer in position to fight their cause because their treasuries and their bargaining rights have been taken over by the white locals, leaving them (Negro members) without representation as officers of the local or as members of the negotiating, grievance or shop committees.

In more than one instance, it has been charged that the International Union has exerted extreme pressure to eliminate (not merge) the Negro local while at the same time trying to shut off protests of discrimination by Negro workers. When one considers that in at least one large cigarette manufacturing center, several officers of the formally all-white locals are at the same time said to be officers of the White Citizens Councils, we may have reason to fear that Negro workers will be eliminated rapidly from these plants and that their loss of seniority rights and exclusion from the skilled categories of employment will not be aggrieved through any affirmative action on the part of a union dominated by arch segregationists.[89]

In fact, few black locals had many assets to covet. A year before it merged, Louisville Negro Local 72, at Philip Morris, was trusteed because it was insolvent. It regained its autonomy, only to be trusteed again and forcibly merged—on the face of it, a quite likely high-handed, but from the national union point of view, understandable action, and one supported by some of its members and former officials.

Mr. Wheeler's charge that integration of locals was directed at silencing them certainly was not successful, even if true. Negro protests continued and the vast federal and state machinery designed to hear such protests, as the research heretofore discussed amply demonstrated, has provided numerous forums and given ample opportunity for frequent and varied complaints.

---

89. John H. Wheeler, "The Impact of Race Relations on Industrial Relations in the South," *Proceedings of the 1964 Spring Meeting*, Industrial Relations Racial Association, 1964, p. 477.

In addition to the two locals with Negro presidents, there are some others with additional Negro officials, but for the most part Negro representation is now confined to lesser jobs like departmental steward. Most locals' bargaining committees are represented by a proportional number of Negroes, but usually, since the great majority of the membership is white, the Negroes can be easily defeated on any issue before the bargaining committee.

The experience of Negroes in the integrated locals such as that at the Lorillard works in Greensboro shows how Negroes often find that local union integration can change nothing. It is likewise certain that integration has meant a decided loss of convention representation to the black workers who now comprise about 20 percent of TWIU's membership.

In point of fact, the resolution of the segregation pattern in the tobacco industry depends primarily on the integration of the segregated seniority lists and not on the integration of the locals. This is not to say that these two areas do not go hand in hand but only to point out that the heart of the problem has been the segregated employment and seniority systems. Government pressure and court cases would appear to have ended the latter, and mitigated the former. The problems of shrinking employment resulting from the impact of automation and declining consumer demand would, however, seem to insure that change occurs slowly in most locations.

Within this context, the TWIU remains a relatively minor influence. It is not a large nor a strong union; its locals are relatively independent. Since the one-man rule of E. Lewis Evans was ended in 1940, the TWIU has operated under a constitution which gives national officials very limited power. Local unions are the bargaining agents and hold the real power. Local white leadership, directly dependent on white membership for continuation in office are not, and are rarely likely to be, as concerned with equal rights as are national leaders. The latter are anxious to avoid divisive racial problems which weaken their union; the former often see their job as one of preserving the rights and hegemony of their constituents. The national leaders have attempted to give some constructive leadership to integration and have had some success. Their lack of power, the declining employment, and the long history of segregation and discrimination in the industry seem to limit both their influence and the results achieved even with the best of intentions.

CHAPTER V

The Determinants of Change

Integration occurred in the tobacco industry at the lowest ebb of Negro employment. Integration has caused few problems. Temporary boycotts of cafeterias occurred, but did not persist. The fact that the work is not highly skilled—and indeed, largely low skilled—precluded major problems of qualification.

As the court noted in the *Quarles* case, seasonal stemmery employees are likely to be marginal workers, and upgrading of these will continue to be a problem for years. Yet much of the work in the former all-Negro departments is equal in skill to that in the former all-white departments. If the racial-occupational segregation pattern ever had a rationale other than segregation and discrimination, it has not been apparent since the stemmeries were mechanized in the 1930's.

There are thus few problems worth reviewing which have not been sufficiently examined in previous chapters. It is, however, appropriate to note again the basic factors which have affected Negro employment in the industry.

THE ORIGIN AND LOCATION OF THE INDUSTRY

The southern location and the use of Negro slaves in tobacco plants set the stage for continued Negro employment in the industry. Then the development of the cigarette machine in the post-Civil War reconstruction era led to the racial-occupational segregation pattern which was religiously adhered to even in the last major northern plant. Custom dictated the labor utilization pattern and custom was institutionalized, first by management, then by union and management. This went on generally without question, at least until World War II, with no more than token change to 1960. Meanwhile, the employment base of Negroes eroded, but neither management nor union opted for change until government action compelled, or seemed about to compel, such change.

THE DEMAND FOR LABOR

Tobacco was never a large employer, and is now a small one. The demand for labor is likely to shrink rather than expand in the future. Because the industry could always obtain ample white labor, its limited propensity to open up all-white departments to Negroes was never encouraged. In Richmond and Petersburg, Virginia, the demand of higher paying industries has siphoned off the white labor supply and afforded Negroes additional opportunities in the expanding Philip Morris and Brown & Williamson plants. Automation and declining demand in other plants have had the opposite effect, and, for the total industry, employment is expected to decline.

The tobacco industry has been a prime example of the manner in which technological advancement combined with discriminatory employment practices adversely affect Negroes. The greatly reduced proportion of Negroes in the industry is the direct result of mechanization and automation in the stemmeries and other formerly all-black departments combined with the denial to Negroes of opportunities to work in formerly all-white areas. As a result, the industry, which once had a preponderance of Negroes, now is about 25 percent black at most.

GOVERNMENT PRESSURE

That government pressure was needed to alter the status quo is indisputable. Except for some movement at Reynolds, the first breaks came as a result of government committee actions—the Nixon Committee in the late 1950's, the PCEEO and the OFCC later. Government pressure and law suits pursuant to Title VII of the Civil Rights Act of 1964 have clearly precluded continued reliance on a discriminatory seniority system.

Government action has not always been so helpful. The minimum wage laws and regulations, commencing with the National Industrial Recovery Act in 1933 and the Fair Labor Standards Act of 1938, resulted in the continued search for, and installation of, machinery to replace hand labor. The government did not give due heed to the impact of such wage determination. Certainly, minimum wages hurried the displacement process.

Government policy also rushed through the integration of formerly segregated local unions in the simplistic view that such integration would automatically reduce discrimination. The long fight of the black Liggett & Myers local to win a superior *quid pro quo*, the paucity of Negro local union officials in the integrated locals, and the adherence of some integrated locals to a discriminatory departmental seniority system, all indicate that this governmental policy was more concerned with appearance than substance. And the attempt of the Equal Employment Opportunity Commission to reinvestigate the Liggett & Myers settlement is a prime example of duplication and waste of scarce government resources.

Again, however, with all its limitations, one must credit government action with breaking the racial-occupational segregation pattern. Without such pressure, or the threat thereof, it is difficult to believe that much of the progress which has occurred would have materialized.

MANAGERIAL ACTION

With one exception, management has been slow to lead in this industry. Reluctant to antagonize the southern community or to upset existing collective bargaining relationships, tobacco management stayed with the status quo until pushed or prodded by government.

Reynolds took more leadership. Consciously nonunion, it has developed an outstanding personnel department which has great prestige in the company and has been traditionally alert for change. Seeing change in the offing, Reynolds moved carefully, intelligently, and thoroughly when the opening of its new Whitaker Park facility provided the opportunity. The company's leadership in the community, again a function of its alert policies, aided its integration program. Having allowed its proportion of Negro employees to decline precipitously, as did other companies, Reynolds has vigorously attempted to offset the inroads of automation in order to reverse this trend. As the industry leader in sales and market share, it may not suffer in the future the job declines which could well beset the industry, a fact which should be helpful to Negro employment.

Philip Morris also deserves special mention for its successful efforts in both Louisville and Richmond, and its relatively early action to eliminate past discriminatory practices. Negro advancement now is likely to be greatest at the above facilities of Philip Morris and those of Brown & Williamson at Petersburg. A large Negro representation in the labor force and expanding demand have aided these companies in improving their racial policies and Negro representation in their plants.

UNION POLICY

Until recently the Tobacco Workers' International Union accepted and institutionalized the racial-occupational segregation pattern. TWIU negotiations have raised the wages of Negroes, but the union did little on its own initiative to halt the decline of Negro jobs while Negroes were laid off and whites hired, nor otherwise to alter the racial-occupational segregation pattern, nor to eliminate discriminatory practices. Instead TWIU policies institutionalized the existing structure and added barriers against Negro employment opportunity. The strong TWIU support to eliminate racially segregated locals came only after Negroes were no longer a majority in any plant.

Actually, as was pointed out in the previous chapter, the national TWIU is not strong and the locals have considerable independence. In such a situation, the views of the dominant white majority are likely to prevail, and the rights of black minorities are frequently ignored. Negro local union officials and leaders have therefore sought redress outside of their union—through civil rights and government agencies. They saw the TWIU as antagonistic to their aspirations, and the union in turn was usually arguing for the status quo, although the international officials strongly supported the integration of locals, and sought to develop a constructive solution in the final resolution of the big Liggett & Myers case.

Union organization has hindered Negro job opportunities in one other way. The craft unions are strong among maintenance crews in many tobacco plants. Where this occurs, Negroes have found an additional barrier to the many which inhibit opportunities in such jobs.

CONCLUDING REMARKS

The racial-occupational segregation pattern in the tobacco industry endured for nearly a century. When it was finally broken, Negroes, who had once dominated the industry's factory employment, held only 25 percent of the jobs, an all-time low. The industry's sales are not increasing as consumers become wary of the influence of smoking on health and the dangers of crippling disease; moreover, automation is continuing to affect jobs. Thus new opportunities for Negroes may not result in substantial change because of declining labor demand. The only offsetting factors are the strong affirmative action program at the

Reynolds complex in Winston-Salem, the continued affirmative action and expansion of both sales and employment at the Philip Morris plants in Richmond and Louisville, and the increased utilization of Negroes at the Petersburg facility of Brown & Williamson. Since overall employment in the industry, however, is likely to decline, opportunities for Negroes may depend strongly on the extent to which whites prefer jobs elsewhere. Negroes are therefore likely to have their greatest opportunities in the tobacco industry in cities like Louisville and Richmond where a multitude of industries competes for labor and where many often pay considerably more than does the tobacco industry.

Appendix A

ESTIMATE OF NEGRO EMPLOYMENT FOR 1960

The U. S. Census of Population for 1960 did not list the Negroes separately from the whites for tobacco manufacturing in North Carolina, Kentucky, and Virginia as in the previous census. Therefore, a possible minimum and maximum number of Negroes in this industry was obtained in the following manner: Table 127 for each state listed the male and female workers for each detailed industry, one of which was tobacco manufacturing. Table 129 broke down the employed persons by white and Negro only by industry, not detailed industry. Therefore, in the category of "All Other Non-Durable Goods" industries in Table 129, "Tobacco Manufacturing" was combined with "Leather: Tanned, Cured, and Finished" and "Leather Products, except Footwear."

From Table 127, the total labor force in tobacco manufacturing was ascertained by combining the male and female totals. Likewise, total employment figures were computed for the two leather categories. Then, by assuming that all employees in the two leather categories were Negroes, a minimum number of Negroes available for the tobacco manufacturing category was computed. Total Negroes, male and female, from Table 129, less the total employment for the two leather occupations, resulted in a minimum possible number of Negroes in tobacco manufacturing.

This same approach was used to determine the maximum possible number of Negroes in tobacco manufacturing by making an assumption that all the employees in the two leather groups were white.

Even though the figures in Table A-1 are not exact, in comparison with the 1950 data, a definite trend is observable regardless of whether the 1960 minimum or maximum figures for the Negro are used in the comparison.

The wide range of Negroes in Kentucky in 1960 is due to the low total of Negroes (1,298) and the relatively high number of workers (440) in the two leather categories.

TABLE A-1. *Tobacco Industry*
Total and Negro Employment
Kentucky, North Carolina, and Virginia, 1950 and 1960

	1950			1960				
	Total	Negro	Percent Negro	Total	Negro (Minimum)	Negro (Maximum)	Percent Negro (Minimum)	Percent Negro (Maximum)
Kentucky	7,457	1,328	17.8					
North Carolina	22,251	9,407	42.3					
Virginia	10,955	4,384	40.0					
Total	40,663	15,119	37.2					
Total—Kentucky, North Carolina, and Virginia								
All other nondurable goods				51,174	13,130	13,130		
Less: Leather, tanned, curried, & finished				1,332				
Leather products except footwear				932		0		
Subtotal				2,264		2,264		
Total tobacco manufacturing				48,910	10,866	13,130	22.2	26.8

Kentucky

All other nondurable goods	9,782	1,298	1,298		
Less: Leather, tanned, etc.	351				
Leather products	89				
Subtotal	440	440	0		
Total tobacco manufacturing	9,342	858	1,298	9.2	13.9

North Carolina

All other nondurable goods	28,054	8,666	8,666		
Less: Leather, tanned, etc.	337				
Leather products	252				
Subtotal	589	589	0		
Total tobacco manufacturing	27,465	8,077	8,666	29.4	31.6

Virginia

All other nondurable goods	13,338	3,166	3,166		
Less: Leather, tanned, etc.	644				
Leather products	591				
Subtotal	1,235	1,235	0		
Total tobacco manufacturing	12,103	1,931	3,166	15.9	26.2

Source: *U. S. Census of Population:*

1950: Vol. II, *Characteristics of the Population,* State Volumes, Table 83.
1960: PC(1)D, *Characteristics of the Population,* State Volumes, Tables 127 and 129.

Appendix B

Basic Statistical Tables, 1964, 1966, and 1968

TABLE B-1. *Tobacco Industry*

Employment by Race, Sex, and Occupational Group

5 Companies

Kentucky, 1964

Occupational Group	All Employees			Male			Female		
	Total	Negro	Percent Negro	Total	Negro	Percent Negro	Total	Negro	Percent Negro
Officials and managers	589	5	0.8	585	5	0.9	4	—	—
Professionals	106	1	0.9	102	—	—	4	1	25.0
Technicians	190	2	1.1	117	—	—	73	2	2.7
Sales workers	580	15	2.6	580	15	2.6	—	—	—
Office and clerical	782	24	3.1	260	4	1.5	522	20	3.8
Total white collar	2,247	47	2.1	1,644	24	1.5	603	23	3.8
Craftsmen	870	7	0.8	854	7	0.8	16	—	—
Operatives	4,178	236	5.6	2,032	161	7.9	2,146	75	3.5
Laborers	2,372	539	22.7	1,518	380	25.0	854	159	18.6
Service workers	414	149	36.0	288	116	40.3	126	33	26.2
Total blue collar	7,834	931	11.9	4,692	664	14.2	3,142	267	8.5
Total	10,081	978	9.7	6,336	688	10.9	3,745	290	7.7

Source: Data in author's possession.

TABLE B-2. *Tobacco Industry*
Employment by Race, Sex, and Occupational Group
5 Companies
North Carolina, 1964

Occupational Group	All Employees			Male			Female		
	Total	Negro	Percent Negro	Total	Negro	Percent Negro	Total	Negro	Percent Negro
Officials and managers	1,801	10	0.6	1,797	10	0.6	4	—	—
Professionals	484	2	0.4	468	1	0.2	16	1	6.2
Technicians	777	14	1.8	686	11	1.6	91	3	3.3
Sales workers	1,337	23	1.7	1,290	23	1.8	47	—	—
Office and clerical	2,001	44	2.2	815	22	2.7	1,186	22	1.9
Total white collar	6,400	93	1.5	5,056	67	1.3	1,344	26	1.9
Craftsmen	3,030	65	2.1	2,890	65	2.2	140	—	—
Operatives	9,091	1,384	15.2	5,821	1,055	18.1	3,270	329	10.1
Laborers	7,065	3,834	54.3	3,856	3,046	79.0	3,209	788	24.6
Service workers	1,214	961	79.2	991	742	74.9	223	219	98.2
Total blue collar	20,400	6,244	30.6	13,558	4,908	36.2	6,842	1,336	19.5
Total	26,800	6,337	23.6	18,614	4,975	26.7	8,186	1,362	16.6

Source: Data in author's possession.

TABLE B-3. *Tobacco Industry*

Employment by Race, Sex, and Occupational Group

5 Companies

Virginia, 1964

Occupational Group	All Employees			Male			Female		
	Total	Negro	Percent Negro	Total	Negro	Percent Negro	Total	Negro	Percent Negro
Officials and managers	416	10	2.4	416	10	2.4	—	—	—
Professionals	238	3	1.3	212	3	1.4	26	—	—
Technicians	203	2	1.0	125	2	1.6	78	—	—
Sales workers	—	—	—	—	—	—	—	—	—
Office and clerical	522	23	4.4	205	14	6.8	317	9	2.8
Total white collar	1,379	38	2.8	958	29	3.0	421	9	2.1
Craftsmen	1,050	10	1.0	1,016	10	1.0	34	—	—
Operatives	4,803	748	15.6	2,286	567	24.8	2,517	181	7.2
Laborers	2,948	1,553	52.7	1,754	1,110	63.3	1,194	443	37.1
Service workers	365	245	67.1	329	211	64.1	36	34	94.4
Total blue collar	9,166	2,556	27.9	5,385	1,898	35.2	3,781	658	17.4
Total	10,545	2,594	24.6	6,343	1,927	30.4	4,202	667	15.9

Source: Data in author's possession.

TABLE B-4. *Tobacco Industry*
Employment by Race, Sex, and Occupational Group
5 Companies
Kentucky, 1966

Occupational Group	All Employees			Male			Female		
	Total	Negro	Percent Negro	Total	Negro	Percent Negro	Total	Negro	Percent Negro
Officials and managers	749	7	0.9	731	7	1.0	18	—	—
Professionals	123	1	0.8	117	—	—	6	1	16.7
Technicians	192	3	1.6	107	2	1.9	85	1	1.2
Sales workers	588	17	2.9	588	17	2.9	—	—	—
Office and clerical	870	26	3.0	296	6	2.0	574	20	3.5
Total white collar	2,522	54	2.1	1,839	32	1.7	683	22	3.2
Craftsmen	784	8	1.0	784	8	1.0	—	—	—
Operatives	4,471	392	8.8	2,243	286	12.8	2,228	106	4.8
Laborers	3,344	1,012	30.3	1,946	589	30.3	1,398	423	30.3
Service workers	453	160	35.3	304	105	34.5	149	55	36.9
Total blue collar	9,052	1,572	17.4	5,277	988	18.7	3,775	584	15.5
Total	11,574	1,626	14.0	7,116	1,020	14.3	4,458	606	13.6

Source: Data in author's possession.

TABLE B-5. Tobacco Industry
Employment by Race, Sex, and Occupational Group
5 Companies
North Carolina, 1966

Occupational Group	All Employees			Male			Female		
	Total	Negro	Percent Negro	Total	Negro	Percent Negro	Total	Negro	Percent Negro
Officials and managers	1,597	13	0.8	1,594	13	0.8	3	—	—
Professionals	441	3	0.7	427	2	0.5	14	1	7.1
Technicians	611	15	2.5	552	14	2.5	59	1	1.7
Sales workers	1,393	26	1.9	1,320	24	1.8	73	2	2.7
Office and clerical	1,521	45	3.0	547	25	4.6	974	20	2.1
Total white collar	5,563	102	1.8	4,440	78	1.8	1,123	24	2.1
Craftsmen	2,804	65	2.3	2,703	65	2.4	101	—	—
Operatives	8,981	1,448	16.1	5,833	1,203	20.6	3,148	245	7.8
Laborers	6,563	3,570	54.4	3,679	2,812	76.4	2,884	758	26.3
Service workers	1,076	842	78.3	856	634	74.1	220	208	94.5
Total blue collar	19,424	5,925	30.5	13,071	4,714	36.1	6,353	1,211	19.1
Total	24,987	6,027	24.1	17,511	4,792	27.4	7,476	1,235	16.5

Source: Data in author's possession.

TABLE B-6. *Tobacco Industry*
Employment by Race, Sex, and Occupational Group
5 Companies
Virginia, 1966

Occupational Group	All Employees			Male			Female		
	Total	Negro	Percent Negro	Total	Negro	Percent Negro	Total	Negro	Percent Negro
Officials and managers	675	17	2.5	614	17	2.8	61	—	—
Professionals	274	4	1.5	247	4	1.6	27	—	—
Technicians	237	5	2.1	143	4	2.8	94	1	1.1
Sales workers	5	1	20.0	5	1	20.0	—	—	—
Office and clerical	500	29	5.8	175	17	9.7	325	12	3.7
Total white collar	1,691	56	3.3	1,184	43	3.6	507	13	2.6
Craftsmen	954	13	1.4	954	13	1.4	—	—	—
Operatives	4,734	830	17.5	2,291	597	26.1	2,443	233	9.5
Laborers	3,055	1,532	50.1	1,834	1,114	60.7	1,221	418	34.2
Service workers	387	260	67.2	352	226	64.2	35	34	97.1
Total blue collar	9,130	2,635	28.9	5,431	1,950	35.9	3,699	685	18.5
Total	10,821	2,691	24.9	6,615	1,993	30.1	4,206	698	16.6

Source: Data in author's possession.

TABLE B-7. *Tobacco Industry*
Employment by Race, Sex, and Occupational Group
5 Companies
Kentucky, 1968

Occupational Group	All Employees			Male			Female		
	Total	Negro	Percent Negro	Total	Negro	Percent Negro	Total	Negro	Percent Negro
Officials and managers	821	15	1.8	787	15	1.9	34	—	—
Professionals	180	—	—	166	—	—	14	—	—
Technicians	214	3	1.4	106	1	0.9	108	2	1.9
Sales workers	—	—	—	—	—	—	—	—	—
Office and clerical	949	38	4.0	315	8	2.5	634	30	4.7
Total white collar	2,164	56	2.6	1,374	24	1.7	790	32	4.1
Craftsmen	971	6	0.6	971	6	0.6	—	—	—
Operatives	5,841	593	10.2	3,102	384	12.4	2,739	209	7.6
Laborers	3,712	1,035	27.9	2,195	613	27.9	1,517	422	27.8
Service workers	477	176	36.9	373	123	33.0	104	53	51.0
Total blue collar	11,001	1,810	16.5	6,641	1,126	17.0	4,360	684	15.7
Total	13,165	1,866	14.2	8,015	1,150	14.3	5,150	716	13.9

Source: Data in author's possession.

TABLE B-8. *Tobacco Industry*
Employment by Race, Sex, and Occupational Group
5 Companies
North Carolina, 1968

Occupational Group	All Employees			Male			Female		
	Total	Negro	Percent Negro	Total	Negro	Percent Negro	Total	Negro	Percent Negro
Officials and managers	1,674	21	1.3	1,668	21	1.3	6	—	—
Professionals	621	6	1.0	576	4	0.7	45	2	4.4
Technicians	689	23	3.3	615	20	3.3	74	3	4.1
Sales workers	1,319	41	3.1	1,272	41	3.2	47	—	—
Office and clerical	1,834	58	3.2	584	18	3.1	1,250	40	3.2
Total white collar	6,137	149	2.4	4,715	104	2.2	1,422	45	3.2
Craftsmen	2,847	80	2.8	2,820	80	2.8	27	—	—
Operatives	9,122	1,720	18.9	5,484	1,344	24.5	3,638	376	10.3
Laborers	5,989	3,227	53.9	3,751	2,632	70.2	2,238	595	26.6
Service workers	1,061	649	61.2	866	498	57.5	195	151	77.4
Total blue collar	19,019	5,676	29.8	12,921	4,554	35.2	6,098	1,122	18.4
Total	25,156	5,825	23.2	17,636	4,658	26.4	7,520	1,167	15.5

Source: Data in the author's possession.

TABLE B-9.   Tobacco Industry
Employment by Race, Sex, and Occupational Group
5 Companies
Virginia, 1968

Occupational Group	All Employees			Male			Female		
	Total	Negro	Percent Negro	Total	Negro	Percent Negro	Total	Negro	Percent Negro
Officials and managers	831	28	3.4	792	28	3.5	39	—	—
Professionals	165	1	0.6	142	1	0.7	23	—	—
Technicians	221	8	3.6	163	8	4.9	58	—	—
Sales workers	—	—	—	—	—	—	—	—	—
Office and clerical	622	37	5.9	228	16	7.0	394	21	5.3
Total white collar	1,839	74	4.0	1,325	53	4.0	514	21	4.1
Craftsmen	1,023	21	2.1	1,023	21	2.1	—	—	—
Operatives	4,917	1,125	22.9	2,544	853	33.5	2,373	272	11.5
Laborers	3,426	1,913	55.8	2,153	1,419	65.9	1,273	494	38.8
Service workers	435	265	60.9	393	241	61.3	42	24	57.1
Total blue collar	9,801	3,324	33.9	6,113	2,534	41.5	3,688	790	21.4
Total	11,640	3,398	29.2	7,438	2,587	34.8	4,202	811	19.3

Source: Data in author's possession.

Index